Proust and Signs

THEORY OUT OF BOUNDS

Edited by
Sandra Buckley
Michael Hardt
Brian Massumi

Proust and Signs

THE COMPLETE TEXT

Gilles Deleuze

Translated by Richard Howard

THEORY OUT OF BOUNDS, VOLUME 17

University of Minnesota Press

Minneapolis

English language edition first published by George Braziller, Inc., 1972.
English translation copyright 1972 by George Braziller, Inc.

Originally published in French under the title *Proust et les Signes*, copyright
1964 Presses Universitaires de France.

Published by the University of Minnesota Press
111 Third Avenue South, Suite 290
Minneapolis, MN 55401-2520
http://www.upress.umn.edu

Library of Congress Cataloging-in-Publication Data

Deleuze, Gilles.
    [Proust et les signes. English]
    Proust and signs : the complete text / Gilles Deleuze ; translated by
Richard Howard.
        p.   cm. — (Theory out of bounds ; v. 17)
    ISBN 0-8166-3257-X (hc: alk. paper) — ISBN 0-8166-3258-8 (pbk)
    1. Proust, Marcel, 1871–1922. A la recherche du temps perdu.
I. Title. II. Series.
PQ2631.R63 A78613   2000
843'.912 — dc21   99-050616

11 10 09 08 07 06 05 04   10 9 8 7 6 5 4 3 2

Contents

Translator's Note

In the course of this study, the title of Proust's work will be given as *In Search of Lost Time,* and Deleuze's frequent reference to "the Search" comprehends both Proust's work and the subject of it. Citations refer to the volumes and pages of the three-volume edition of *A la Recherche du temps perdu,* published in the Bibliothèque de la Pléiade, from which all translations are by Richard Howard.

Preface to the Complete Text

The first part of this book concerns the emission and the interpretation of signs as presented in *In Search of Lost Time*. The other part, added to the 1972 edition as a single chapter, deals with a different problem: the production and the multiplication of signs themselves, from the point of view of the composition of the Search. This second part is now divided into chapters, in a desire for greater clarity. It is completed by a text first published in 1973 and subsequently revised.

G.D.

Preface to the 1972 Edition

This book considers Proust's entire work as commanded by an experience of signs that mobilizes the involuntary and the unconscious: whence the Search as interpretation. But interpretation is the converse of a production of signs themselves. The work of art not only interprets and not only emits signs to be interpreted; it *produces* them, by determinable procedures. Proust himself conceives his work as an apparatus or a machine capable of functioning effectively, *producing signs of different orders*, which will have an effect on the reader. It is this viewpoint I have attempted to analyze in chapter 8, added to the original edition.

G.D.

Works by Proust

Original French Title	English Translation Title
Albertine disparue	The Fugitive
Le Côté de Guermantes, 1	The Guermantes Way
Le Côté de Guermantes, 2	
Le Côté de Guermantes, 3	
Du côté du chez Swann, 1	Swann's Way
Du côté du chez Swann, 2	
A l'ombre des jeunes filles en fleur, 1	Within a Budding Grove
A l'ombre des jeunes filles en fleur, 2	
A l'ombre des jeunes filles en fleur, 3	
La Prisonnière, 1	The Captive
La Prisonnière, 2	
Sodome et Gomorrhe, 1	Sodom and Gomorrah
Sodome et Gomorrhe, 2	
Le Temps retrouvé, 1	Time Regained
Le Temps retrouvé, 2	

Part I. The Signs

CHAPTER 1

The Types of Signs

What constitutes the unity of *In Search of Lost Time*? We know, at least, what does not. It is not recollection, memory, even involuntary memory. What is essential to the Search is not in the madeleine or the cobblestones. On the one hand, the Search is not simply an effort of recall, an exploration of memory: search, *recherche*, is to be taken in the strong sense of the term, as we say "the search for truth." On the other hand, Lost Time is not simply "time past"; it is also time wasted, lost track of. Consequently, memory intervenes as a means of search, of investigation, but not the most profound means; and time past intervenes as a structure of time, but not the most profound structure. In Proust, the steeples of Martinville and Vinteuil's little phrase, which cause no memory, no resurrection of the past to intervene, will always prevail over the madeleine and the cobblestones of Venice, which depend on memory and thereby still refer to a "material explanation" (III, 375).

What is involved is not an exposition of involuntary memory, but the narrative of an apprenticeship: more precisely, the apprenticeship of a man of letters. (III, 907). The Méséglise Way and the Guermantes Way are not so much the sources of memory as the raw materials, the lines of an apprenticeship. They are the two ways of a "formation." Proust constantly insists on this: at one moment or another, the hero does not yet know this or that; he will learn it later on. He is under a certain illusion, which he will ultimately discard. Whence the movement of disappointments and revelations, which imparts its rhythm to the Search as a whole. One might invoke Proust's Platonism: to learn is still to remember. But however important its role, memory intervenes only as the means of an apprenticeship that transcends recollection both by its goals and by its principles. The Search is oriented to the future, not to the past.

Learning is essentially concerned with *signs*. Signs are the object of a temporal apprenticeship, not of an abstract knowledge. To learn is first of all to consider a substance, an object, a being as if it emitted signs to be deciphered, interpreted. There is no apprentice who is not "the Egyptologist" of something. One becomes a carpenter only by becoming sensitive to the signs of wood, a physician by becoming sensitive to the signs of disease. Vocation is always predestination with regard to signs. Everything that teaches us something emits signs; every act of learning is an interpretation of signs or hieroglyphs. Proust's work is based not on the exposition of memory, but on the apprenticeship to signs.

From them it derives its unity and also its astonishing pluralism. The word sign, *signe*, is one of the most frequent in the work, notably in the final systematization that constitutes Time Regained (*Le Temps Retrouvé*). The Search is presented as the exploration of different worlds of signs that are organized in circles and intersect at certain points, for the signs are specific and constitute the substance of one world or another. We see this at once in the secondary characters: Norpois and the diplomatic code, *on different worlds, and how signs differ in each*

Saint-Loup and the signs of strategy, Cottard and medical symptoms. A man can be skillful at deciphering the signs of one realm but remain a fool in every other case: thus Cottard, a great clinician. Further, in a shared realm, the worlds are partitioned off: the Verdurin signs have no currency among the Guermantes; conversely Swann's style or Charlus's hieroglyphs do not pass among the Verdurins. The worlds are unified by their formation of sign systems emitted by persons, objects, substances; we discover no truth, we learn nothing except by deciphering and interpreting. But the plurality of worlds is such that these signs are not of the same kind, do not have the same way of appearing, do not allow themselves to be deciphered in the same manner, do not have an identical relation with their meaning. The hypothesis that the signs form both the unity and the plurality of the Search must be verified by considering the worlds in which the hero participates directly.

The Signs

The first world of the Search is the world of, precisely, ⟨. worldliness. There is no milieu that emits and concentrates so many signs, in such reduced space, at so great a rate. It is true that these signs themselves are not homogeneous. At one and the same moment they are differentiated, not only according to classes but according to even more fundamental "families of mind." From one moment to the next, they evolve, crystallize, or give way to other signs. Thus the apprentice's task is to understand why someone is "received" in a certain world, why someone ceases to be so, what signs do the worlds obey, which signs are legislators, and which high priests. In Proust's work, *worldly = action + thought*

Charlus is the most prodigious emitter of signs, by his worldly power, his pride, his sense of theater, his face, and his voice. But Charlus, driven by love, is nothing at the Verdurins', and even in his own world he will end by being nothing when its implicit laws have changed. What then is the unity of the worldly signs? A greeting from the Duc de Guermantes is to be interpreted, and the risks of error are as great in such an interpretation as in a diagnosis. The same is true of a gesture of Mme Verdurin.

The worldly sign appears as the replacement of an action or a thought. It stands for action and for thought. It is therefore a sign that does not refer to something else, to a transcendent signification or to an ideal content, but has usurped the supposed value of its meaning. This is why worldliness, judged from the viewpoint of actions, appears to be disappointing and cruel, and from the viewpoint of thought, it appears stupid. One does not think and one does not act, but one makes signs. Nothing funny is said at the Verdurins', and Mme Verdurin does not laugh; but Cottard makes a sign that he is saying something funny, Mme Verdurin makes a sign that she is laughing, and her sign is so perfectly emitted that M. Verdurin, not to be outdone, seeks in his turn for an appropriate mimicry. Mme de Guermantes has a heart that is often hard, a mind that is often weak, but she always has charming signs. She does not act for her friends, she does not think with them, she makes signs to them. The worldly sign does not refer to something, it "stands for" it, claims to be equivalent to its meaning. It anticipates action as it does thought, annuls thought as it does action, and declares itself adequate: whence its stereotyped aspect and its vacu-

ity. We must not thereby conclude that such signs are neg-
ligible. The apprenticeship would be imperfect and even
impossible if it did not pass through them. These signs
are empty, but this emptiness confers upon them a ritual
perfection, a kind of formalism we do not encounter elsewhere. The worldly signs are the only ones capable of
causing a kind of nervous exaltation, expressing the effect
upon us of the persons who are capable of producing them
(II, 547–52).

2. The second circle is that of love. The Charlus-Jupien encounter makes the reader a party to the most prodigious
exchange of signs. To fall in love is to individualize someone by the signs he bears or emits. It is to become sensitive to these signs, to undergo an apprenticeship to them
(thus the slow individualization of Albertine in the group
of young girls). It may be that friendship is nourished on
observation and conversation, but love is born from and
nourished on silent interpretation. The beloved appears
as a sign, a "soul"; the beloved expresses a possible world
unknown to us, implying, enveloping, imprisoning a world
that must be deciphered, that is, interpreted. What is involved, here, is a plurality of worlds; the pluralism of love
does not concern only the multiplicity of loved beings,
but the multiplicity of souls or worlds in each of them. To
love is to try to *explicate*, to *develop* these unknown worlds
that remain enveloped within the beloved. This is why it
is so easy for us to fall in love with women who are not of
our "world" nor even our type. It is also why the loved
women are often linked to landscapes that we know sufficiently to long for their reflection in a woman's eyes but

are then reflected from a viewpoint so mysterious that they become virtually inaccessible, unknown landscapes: Albertine envelops, incorporates, amalgamates "the beach and the breaking waves." How can we gain access to a landscape that is no longer the one we see, but on the contrary the one in which we are seen? "If she had seen me, what could I have meant to her? From what universe did she select me?" (I, 794).

There is, then, a contradiction of love. We cannot interpret the signs of a loved person without proceeding into worlds that have not waited for us in order to take form, that formed themselves with other persons, and in which we are at first only an object among the rest. The lover wants his beloved to devote to him her preferences, her gestures, her caresses. But the beloved's gestures, at the very moment they are addressed to us, still express that unknown world that excludes us. The beloved gives us signs of preference; but because these signs are the same as those that express worlds to which we do not belong, each preference by which we profit draws the image of the *possible world* in which others might be or are preferred. "All at once his jealousy, as if it were the shadow of his love, was completed by the double of this new smile that she had given him that very evening and that, conversely now, mocked Swann and was filled with love for someone else.... So he came to regret each pleasure he enjoyed with her, each caress they devised whose delight he had been so indiscreet as to reveal to her, each grace he discerned in her, for he knew that a moment later they would constitute new instruments of his torment" (I, 276). The contradiction of love consists of this: the means we

Laws of love

count on to preserve us from jealousy are the very means that develop that jealousy, giving it a kind of autonomy, of independence with regard to our love.

The first law of love is subjective: subjectively, jealousy is deeper than love, it contains love's truth. This is because jealousy goes further in the apprehension and interpretation of signs. It is the destination of love, its finality. Indeed, it is inevitable that the signs of a loved person, once we "explicate" them, should be revealed as deceptive: addressed to us, applied to us, they nonetheless express worlds that exclude us and that the beloved will not and cannot make us know. Not by virtue of any particular ill will on the beloved's part, but of a deeper contradiction, which inheres in the nature of love and in the general situation of the beloved. Love's signs are not like the signs of worldliness; they are not empty signs, standing for thought and action. They are deceptive signs that can be addressed to us only by concealing what they express: the origin of unknown worlds, of unknown actions and thoughts that give them a meaning. They do not excite a superficial, nervous exaltation, but the suffering of a deeper exploration. The beloved's lies are the hieroglyphics of love. The interpreter of love's signs is necessarily the interpreter of lies. His fate is expressed in the motto To love without being loved.

What does the lie conceal in love's signs? All the deceptive signs emitted by a loved woman converge upon the same secret world: the world of Gomorrah, which itself no longer depends on this or that woman (though one woman can incarnate it better than another) but is the feminine possibility par excellence, a kind of a priori that jealousy discovers. This is because the world expressed by the loved woman is always a world that excludes us, even when she gives us a mark of preference. But, of all the worlds, which one is the most excluding, the most exclusive? "It was a terrible terra incognita on which I had just landed, a new phase of unsuspected sufferings that was beginning. And yet this deluge of reality that submerges us, if it is real in relation to our timid presuppositions, was nonetheless anticipated by them.... The rival was not like me, the rival's weapons were different; I could not join battle on the same terrain, give Albertine the same pleasures, nor even conceive just what they might be" (II, 1115–20). We interpret all the signs of the loved woman, but, at the end of this painful decipherment, we come up against the sign of Gomorrah as though against the deepest expression of an original feminine reality.

(2) The second law of Proustian love is linked with the first: objectively, heterosexual loves are less profound than homosexual ones; they find their truth in homosexuality. For if it is true that the loved woman's secret is the secret of Gomorrah, the lover's secret is that of Sodom. In analogous circumstances, the hero of the Search surprises Mlle Vinteuil and surprises Charlus (II, 608). But Mlle Vinteuil explicates all loved women, as Charlus implicates all lovers. At the infinity of our loves, there is the original Hermaphrodite. But the Hermaphrodite is not a being capable of reproducing itself. Far from uniting the sexes, it separates them, it is the source from which there continually proceed the two divergent homosexual series, that of Sodom and that of Gomorrah. It is the Hermaphrodite that possesses the key to Samson's prophecy: "The two

sexes shall die, each in a place apart" (II, 616). To the point where heterosexual loves are merely the appearance that covers the destination of each sex, concealing the accursed depth where everything is elaborated. And if the two homosexual series are the most profound, it is still in terms of signs. The characters of Sodom, the characters of Gomorrah compensate by the intensity of the sign for the secret to which they are bound. Of a woman looking at Albertine, Proust writes: "One would have said that she was making signs to her as though with a beacon" (II, 851). The entire world of love extends from the signs revealing deception to the concealed signs of Sodom and of Gomorrah.

The third world is that of sensuous impressions or qualities. It may happen that a sensuous quality gives us a strange joy at the same time that it transmits a kind of imperative. Thus experienced, the quality no longer appears as a property of the object that now possesses it, but as the sign of an *altogether different* object that we must try to decipher, at the cost of an effort that always risks failure. It is as if the quality enveloped, imprisoned the soul of an object other than the one it now designates. We "develop" this quality, this sensuous impression, like a tiny Japanese paper that opens under water and releases the captive form (I, 47). Examples of this kind are the most famous in the Search and accelerate at its end (the final revelation of "time regained" is announced by a multiplication of signs). But whatever the examples—madeleine, steeples, trees, cobblestones, napkin, noise of a spoon or a pipe—we witness the same procedure. First a prodigious

unfolding signs

joy, so that these signs are already distinguished from the preceding ones by their immediate effect. Further, a kind of obligation is felt, the necessity of a mental effort to seek the sign's meaning (yet we may evade this imperative, out of laziness, or else our investigations may fail out of impotence or bad luck, as in the case of the trees). Then, the sign's meaning appears, yielding to us the concealed object—Combray for the madeleine, young girls for the steeples, Venice for the cobblestones....

It is doubtful that the effort of interpretation ends there. For it remains to be explained why, by the solicitation of the madeleine, Combray is not content to rise up again as it was once present (simple association of ideas), but rises up absolutely, in a form that was never experienced, in its "essence" or its eternity. Or, what amounts to the same thing, it remains to be explained why we experience so intense and so particular a joy. In an important text, Proust cites the madeleine as a case of failure: "I had then postponed seeking the profound causes" (III, 867). Yet, the madeleine looked like a real success, from a certain viewpoint: the interpreter had found its meaning, not without difficulty, in the unconscious memory of Combray. The three trees, on the contrary, are a real failure because their meaning is not elucidated. We must then assume that in choosing the madeleine as an example of inadequacy, Proust is aiming at a new stage of interpretation, an ultimate stage.

This is because the sensuous qualities or impressions, even properly interpreted, are not yet in themselves adequate signs. But they are no longer empty signs, giving us a factitious exaltation like the worldly signs. They are no longer deceptive signs that make us suffer, like the signs of love whose real meaning prepares an ever greater pain. These are true signs that immediately give us an extraordinary joy, signs that are fulfilled, affirmative, and joyous. *But they are material signs.* Not simply by their sensuous origin. But their meaning, as it is developed, signifies Combray, young girls, Venice, or Balbec. It is not only their origin, it is their explanation, their development that remains material (III, 375). We feel that this Balbec, that this Venice . . . do not rise up as the product of an association of ideas, but in person and in their essence. Yet we are not ready to understand what this ideal essence is, nor why we feel so much joy. "The taste of the little madeleine had reminded me of Combray. But why had the images of Combray and of Venice, at the one moment and at the other, given such a certainty of joy, adequate, with no further proofs, to make death itself a matter of indifference to me?" (III, 867).

At the end of the Search, the interpreter understands what had escaped him in the case of the madeleine or even of the steeples: that the material meaning is nothing without an ideal essence that it incarnates. The mistake is to suppose that the hieroglyphs represent "only material objects" (III, 878). But what now permits the interpreter to go further is that meanwhile the problem of art has been raised and has received a solution. Now the world of art is the ultimate world of signs, and these signs, as though *dematerialized*, find their meaning in an ideal essence. Henceforth, the world revealed by art reacts on all the others and notably on the sensuous signs; it integrates them, colors them with an aesthetic meaning, and imbues what was still opaque about them. Then we understand that the sensuous signs *already* referred to an ideal essence that was incarnated in their material meaning. But without art we should not have understood this, nor transcended the law of interpretation that corresponded to the analysis of the madeleine. This is why all the signs converge upon art; all apprenticeships, by the most diverse paths, are already unconscious apprenticeships to art itself. At the deepest level, the essential is in the signs of art.

We have not yet defined them. We ask only the reader's concurrence that Proust's problem is the problem of signs in general and that the signs constitute different worlds, worldly signs, empty signs, deceptive signs of love, sensuous material signs, and lastly the essential signs of art (which transform all the others).

> on worlds and their
> interpretations and
> their difference
>
> all based on the
> essential → art

CHAPTER 2

Signs and Truth

The Search for lost time is in fact a search for truth. If called a search for lost time, it is only to the degree that truth has an essential relation to time. In love as much as in nature or art, it is not pleasure but truth that matters (I, 442). Or rather we have only the pleasures and joys that correspond to the discovery of what is true. The jealous man experiences a tiny thrill of joy when he can decipher one of the beloved's lies, like an interpreter who succeeds in translating a complicated text, even if the translation offers him personally a disagreeable and painful piece of information (I, 282). Again we must understand how Proust defines his own search for truth, how he contrasts it with other kinds of search — scientific or philosophic.

Who is in search of truth? And what does the man who says "I want the truth" mean? Proust does not believe that man, nor even a supposedly pure mind, has by nature a desire for truth, a will-to-truth. We search for truth only when we are determined to do so in terms of a concrete situation, when we undergo a kind of violence that impels us to such a search. Who searches for truth? The jealous man, under the pressure of the beloved's lies. There is always the violence of a sign that forces us into the search, that robs us of peace. The truth is not to be found by affinity, nor by goodwill, but is *betrayed* by involuntary signs (II, 66).

The mistake of philosophy is to presuppose within us a benevolence of thought, a natural love of truth. Thus philosophy arrives at only abstract truths that compromise no one and do not disturb. "The ideas formed by pure intelligence have only a logical truth, a possible truth, their election is arbitrary" (III, 880). They remain gratuitous because they are born of the intelligence that accords them only a possibility and not of a violence or of an encounter that would guarantee their authenticity. The ideas of the intelligence are valid only because of their explicit, hence conventional, signification. There are few themes on which Proust insists as much as on this one: truth is never the product of a prior disposition but the result of a violence in thought. The explicit and conventional significations are never profound; the only profound meaning is the one that is enveloped, implicated in an external sign.

In opposition to the philosophical idea of "method," Proust sets the double idea of "constraint" and of "chance." Truth depends on an encounter with something that forces us to think and to seek the truth. The accident of encounters and the pressure of constraints are Proust's two fundamental themes. Precisely, it is the sign that constitutes the object of an encounter and works this violence upon us. It is the accident of the encounter that guarantees the necessity of what is thought. Fortuitous and inevitable, Proust says: "And I felt that this must be the sign of their authenticity. I had not sought out the two cobblestones of the courtyard where I had stumbled" (III, 879). What is it that the man who says "I want the truth" wants? He wants the truth only when it is constrained and

the encounter = the chance

forced. He wants it only under the rule of an encounter, in relation to such and such a sign. What he wants is to interpret, to decipher, to translate, to find the meaning of the sign. "*Thus I was forced* to restore their meaning to the slightest signs surrounding me, Guermantes, Albertine, Gilberte, Saint-Loup, Balbec, etc." (III, 897).

To seek the truth is to interpret, decipher, explicate. But this "explication" is identified with the development of the sign in itself. This is why the Search is always temporal, and the truth always a truth of time. The final systematization reminds us that Time itself (*le Temps*) is plural. The great distinction in this regard is that between Time lost and Time regained; there are truths of time lost no less than truths of time regained. But, more precisely, it is convenient to distinguish four structures of time, each having its truth. This is because lost time is not only passing time, which alters beings and annihilates what once was, it is also the time one wastes (why must one waste one's time, be worldly, be in love, rather than working and creating a work of art?). And time regained is first of all a time recovered at the heart of time lost, which gives us an image of eternity; but it is also an absolute, original time, an actual eternity that is affirmed in art. Each kind of sign has a line of privileged time that corresponds to it. But there is also the pluralism that multiplies the combinations. Each kind of sign participates in several lines of time; each line of time mingles several kinds of signs.

There are signs that force us to conceive lost time, that is, the passage of time, the annihilation of what was, the alteration of beings. It is a revelation to see again those who were familiar to us, for their faces, no longer a habit, bear in a pure state the signs and effects of time, which has modified this feature, elongated, blurred, or crushed that one. Time, in order to become visible, "seeks bodies and everywhere encounters them, seizes them to cast its magic lantern upon them" (III, 924). A whole gallery of heads appears at the end of the Search, in the salons of the Guermantes. But if we had had the necessary apprenticeship, we would have realized from the start that the worldly signs, by virtue of their vacuity, either betrayed something precarious or else have frozen already, immobilized in order to conceal their alteration. For worldliness, at each moment, is alteration, change. "Fashions change, being themselves born of the need for change" (I, 433). At the end of the Search, Proust shows how the Dreyfus Affair, then the War, but above all Time personified, have profoundly modified society. Far from taking this as the suggestion of the end of a "world," he understands that the very world he had known and loved was already alteration, change, sign, and effect of a lost Time (even the Guermantes have no other permanence than that of their name). Proust does not in the least conceive change as a Bergsonian duration, but as a defection, a race to the grave.

With all the more reason, the signs of love anticipate in some sense their alteration and their annihilation. It is the signs of love that implicate lost time in the purest state. The aging of the salon world is nothing compared with the incredible and inspired aging of Charlus. But here again, Charlus's aging is only the redistribution of his many souls, which were already present in a glance or in

[margin handwritten note: truth changes — who are we to say what is true and what is not]

[bottom handwritten note: change and truth.]

a word of the younger Charlus. If the signs of love and of jealousy carry their own alteration, it is for a simple reason: love unceasingly prepares its own disappearance, acts out its dissolution. The same is true of love as of death, when we imagine we will still be alive enough to see the faces of those who will have lost us. In the same way we imagine that we will still be enough in love to enjoy the regrets of the person we shall have stopped loving. It is quite true that we repeat our past loves; but it is also true that our present love, in all its vivacity, "repeats" the moment of the dissolution or anticipates its own end. Such is the meaning of what we call a scene of jealousy. This repetition oriented to the future, this repetition of the outcome, is what we find in Swann's love of Odette, in the hero's love of Gilberte, of Albertine. Of Saint-Loup, Proust says: "He suffered in advance, without forgetting a single one, all the pains of a dissolution that at other moments he thought he could avoid" (II, 122).

It is more surprising that the sensuous signs, despite their plenitude, can themselves be signs of alteration and of disappearance. Yet Proust cites one case, the boots and the memory of the grandmother, in principle no different from the madeleine or the cobblestones, but which makes us feel a painful disappearance and constitutes the sign of a Time lost forever instead of giving us the plenitude of the Time we regain (II, 755–60). Leaning over to unbutton his boots, he feels something divine; but tears stream from his eyes, involuntary memory brings him the lacerating recollection of his dead grandmother. "It was only at that moment—more than a year after her burial, on account of that anachronism that so often keeps the calendar of facts from coinciding with the calendar of feelings—that I realized she was dead...that I had lost her forever." Why does the involuntary recollection, instead of an image of eternity, afford the acute sentiment of death? It does not suffice to invoke the particular character of the example from which a beloved being rises up once more, nor the guilt the hero feels toward his grandmother. It is in the sensuous sign itself that we must find an ambivalence capable of explaining that it sometimes turns to pain, instead of continuing in joy.

The boot, like the madeleine, causes involuntary memory to intervene: an old sensation tries to superimpose itself, to unite with the present sensation, and extends it over several epochs at once. But it suffices that the present sensation set its "materiality" in opposition to the earlier one for the joy of this superposition to give way to a sentiment of collapse, of irreparable loss, in which the old sensation is pushed back into the depths of lost time. Thus, the fact that the hero regards himself as guilty merely gives the present sensation the power to avoid the embrace of the earlier one. He begins by experiencing the same felicity as in the case of the madeleine, but happiness immediately gives way to the certainty of death and nothingness. There is an ambivalence here, which still remains a possibility of Memory in all the signs in which it intervenes (whence the inferiority of these signs). It is because Memory itself implies "the strange contradiction of survival and of nothingness" (II, 759–60). Even in the madeleine or in the cobblestones, nothingness dawns, this time hidden by the superposition of the two sensations.

In still another manner, the worldly signs, especially the worldly signs but also the signs of love and even the sensuous signs, are the signs of a "lost" time, of time wasted. For it is not reasonable to go into the world, to be in love with mediocre women, nor even to make so many efforts in front of a hawthorn tree. It would be better to frequent profound people, and, above all, to work. The hero of the Search often expresses his disappointment and that of his parents over his incapacity to work, to undertake the literary work he announces (I, 579–81).

But it is an essential result of apprenticeship to reveal to us at the end that there are certain truths of this wasted time. A work undertaken by the effort of the will is nothing; in literature, it can take us only to those truths of the intelligence that lack the mark of necessity and always give the impression that they "might have been" different and differently expressed. Similarly, what a profound and intelligent man says has value in itself, by its manifest content, by its explicit, objective, and elaborated signification; but we shall derive little enough from it, nothing but abstract possibilities, if we have not been able to reach other truths by other paths. These paths are precisely those of the sign. Now a mediocre or stupid person, once we love that person, is richer in signs than the most profound intelligence. The more limited a woman is, the more she compensates by signs, which sometimes betray her and give away a lie, her incapacity to formulate intelligible judgments or to sustain coherent thoughts. Proust says of intellectuals: "The mediocre woman one was amazed to find them loving, enriched their universe much more than any intelligent woman could have done"

(III, 616). There exists an intoxication, afforded by rudimentary natures and substances because they are rich in signs. With the beloved mediocre woman, we return to the origins of humanity, that is, to the moments when signs prevailed over explicit content and hieroglyphs over letters: this woman "communicates" nothing to us, but unceasingly produces signs that must be deciphered.

This is why, when we think we are wasting our time, whether out of snobbery or the dissipation of love, we are often pursuing an obscure apprenticeship until the final revelation of a truth of "lost time." We never know how someone learns; but whatever the way, it is always by the intermediary of signs, by wasting time, and not by the assimilation of some objective content. Who knows how a schoolboy suddenly becomes "good at Latin," which signs (if need be, those of love or even inadmissible ones) have served in his apprenticeship? We never learn from the dictionaries our teachers or our parents lend us. The sign implies in itself a heterogeneity of relation. We never learn by doing *like* someone, but by doing *with* someone, who bears no resemblance to what we are learning. Who knows how a man becomes a great writer? Apropos of Octave, Proust says: "I was no less struck to think that perhaps the most extraordinary masterpieces of our day have come not from the official competitions, from a model academic education à la de Broglie, but from the frequentation of paddocks and of the great bars and cafes" (III, 607).

But wasting time is insufficient. How do we extract the truths of the time we waste—of "lost time"? Why does Proust call these the "truths of the intelligence"? As a matter of fact, they are contrasted with the truths that the in-

telligence discovers when it works by goodwill, applies itself, and refuses to waste time. We have seen in this regard the limitation of strictly intellectual truths: they lack
"necessity." But in art or in literature, when intelligence
supervenes, it is always *after*, not before: "The impression is for the writer what experimentation is for the scientist, with this difference, that in the scientist the work
of the intelligence precedes and in the writer comes after" (III, 880). We must first experience the violent effect
of a sign, and the mind must be "forced" to seek the sign's
meaning. In Proust, thought in general appears in several
guises: memory, desire, imagination, intelligence, faculty
of essences. But in the specific case of time wasted, of "lost
time," it is intelligence and intelligence alone that is capable of supplying the effort of thought, or of interpreting the sign. It is intelligence that finds—provided that
it "comes after." Among all the forms of thought, only the
intelligence extracts truths of this order.

The worldly signs are frivolous, the signs of love and
jealousy, painful. But who would seek the truth if he had
not first learned that a gesture, an intonation, a greeting
must be interpreted? Who would seek the truth if he had
not first suffered the agonies inflicted by the beloved's
lies? The ideas of the intelligence are often "surrogates"
of disappointment (III, 906). Pain forces the intelligence
to seek, just as certain unaccustomed pleasures set memory in motion. It is the responsibility of the intelligence
to understand, and to make us understand, that the most
frivolous signs of worldliness refer to laws, that the most
painful signs of love refer to repetitions. Then we learn
how to make use of other beings: frivolous or cruel, they

understanding truth

*→ proust argues that we only
seek truth from pain / knowlege of*

have "posed before us"; they are no longer anything but the incarnation of themes that transcend them or the fragments of a divinity that is powerless against us. The discovery of the worldly laws gives a meaning to signs that remained insignificant, taken in isolation; but above all, the comprehension of our amorous repetitions changes into joy each of those signs that taken in isolation gave us so much pain. "For to the person we have loved most, we are not so faithful as to ourselves, and we forget that person sooner or later in order to be able, since it is a characteristic of ourselves, to begin to love again" (III, 908). The persons whom we have loved have made us suffer, one by one; but the broken chain they form is a joyous spectacle of intelligence. Then, thanks to intelligence, we discover what we could not know at the start: that we were already apprenticed to signs when we supposed we were wasting our time. We realize that our idle life was indissociable from our work: "My whole life . . . a vocation" (III, 899).

Time wasted, lost time — but also time regained, recovered time. To each kind of sign there doubtless corresponds a privileged line of time. The worldly signs imply chiefly a time wasted; the signs of love envelop especially a time lost. The sensuous signs often afford us the means of regaining time, restore it to us at the heart of time lost. The signs of art, finally, give us a time regained, an original absolute time that includes all the others. But if each sign has its privileged temporal dimension, each also straddles the other lines and participates in the other dimensions of time. Time wasted extends into love and even into the sensuous signs. Time lost appears even in worldliness and also subsists in the signs of sensibility. Time regained reacts in its turn upon time wasted and time lost. And it is in the absolute time of the work of art that all the other dimensions are united and find the truth that corresponds to them. The worlds of signs, the circles of the Search are therefore deployed according to lines of time, veritable *lines of apprenticeship*; but along these lines, they react upon and interfere with each other. Thus the signs do not develop, are not to be explained according to the lines of time without corresponding or symbolizing, without intersecting, without entering into complex combinations that constitute the system of truth.

each level of time
overlaps dimensionally.

Apprenticeship

Proust's work is not oriented to the past and the discoveries of memory, but to the future and the progress of an apprenticeship. What is important is that the hero does not know certain things at the start, gradually learns them, and finally receives an ultimate revelation. Necessarily then, he suffers disappointments: he "believed," he suffered under illusions; the world vacillates in the course of apprenticeship. And still we give a linear character to the development of the Search. As a matter of fact, a certain partial revelation appears in a certain realm of signs, but it is sometimes accompanied by regressions in other realms, it is drowned in a more general disappointment or even reappears elsewhere, always fragile, as long as the revelation of art has not systematized the whole. And at each moment, too, it is possible that a particular disappointment will release laziness again and compromise the whole. Whence the fundamental idea that time forms different series and contains more dimensions than space. What is gained in one is not gained in the other. The Search is given a rhythm not simply by the contributions or sediments of memory, but by series of discontinuous disappointments and also by the means employed to overcome them within each series.

To be sensitive to signs, to consider the world as an object to be deciphered, is doubtless a gift. But this gift risks re-

maining buried in us if we do not make the necessary encounters, and these encounters would remain ineffective
if we failed to overcome certain stock notions. The first of
these is to attribute to the object the signs it bears. Everything encourages us to do so: perception, passion, intelligence, even self-esteem (III, 896). We think that the "object" itself has the secret of the signs it emits. We scrutinize
the object, we return to it in order to decipher the sign.
For the sake of convenience, let us call *objectivism* this tendency that is natural to us or, at least, habitual.

For each of our impressions has two sides: "Half
sheathed in the object, extended in ourselves by another
half that we alone can recognize" (III, 891). Each sign has
two halves: it *designates* an object, it *signifies* something
different. The objective side is the side of pleasure, of immediate delight, and of practice. Taking this way, we have
already sacrificed the "truth" side. We recognize things,
but we never know them. What the sign signifies we identify with the person or object it designates. We miss our
finest encounters, we avoid the imperatives that emanate
from them: to the exploration of encounters we have preferred the facility of recognitions. And when we experience the pleasure of an impression or the splendor of a
sign, we know nothing better to say than "zut, zut, zut"
or, what comes down to the same thing, "bravo, bravo":
expressions that manifest our homage to the object (I,
155–56; III, 892).

Struck by the strange savor, the hero relishes his cup
of tea, takes a second and a third mouthful, as if the object itself might reveal to him the sign's secret. Struck by
a place-name, by a person's name, he dreams first of the

landscapes and people these names designate. Before he knows her, Mme de Guermantes seems to him glamorous because she must possess, he believes, the secret of her name. He imagines her "bathing as in a sunset in the orange light that emanates from that final syllable — antes" (I, 171). And when he sees her: "I told myself that this was indeed the woman whom the name Duchesse de Guermantes *designated* for everyone; the inconceivable life this name *signified* was actually contained by this body" (II, 205). Before he ventures into it, the world seems mysterious to him: he thinks that those who emit signs are also those who understand them and possess their code. During his first loves, he gives "the object" the benefit of all he feels: what seems to him unique in a person also seems to him to belong to this person. So that the first loves are inflected toward avowal, which is precisely the amorous form of homage to the object (to restore to the beloved what one believes belongs to it). "At the time I loved Gilberte, I still believed that love really existed outside ourselves. . . . it seemed to me that if I had, of my own accord, substituted the simulation of indifference for the sweetness of avowal, I would not only have deprived myself of a series of pleasures I had long dreamed of, but I would have fabricated, to my own taste, a factitious and worthless love" (I, 401). Finally, art itself seems to have its secret in objects to be described, things to be designated, characters or places to be observed; and if the hero often doubts his artistic capacities, it is because he knows he is incapable of observing, of listening, of seeing.

"Objectivism" spares no kind of sign. This is because it does not result from a single tendency but groups together a complex of tendencies. To refer a sign to the object that emits it, to attribute to the object the benefit of the sign, is first of all the natural direction of perception or of representation. But it is also the direction of voluntary memory, which recalls things and not signs. It is, further, the direction of pleasure and of practical activity, which count on the possession of things or on the consumption of objects. And in another way, it is the tendency of the intelligence. *The intelligence tends toward objectivity, as perception toward the object.* The intelligence dreams of objective content, of explicit objective significations that it is able, of its own accord, to discover or to receive or to communicate. The intelligence is thus objectivist, as much as perception. It is at the same moment that perception assigns itself the task of apprehending the sensuous object, and intelligence the task of apprehending objective significations. For perception supposes that reality is to be *seen, observed*; but intelligence supposes that truth is to be *spoken, formulated.* The hero of the Search does not know at the start of his apprenticeship "that the truth has no need to be spoken in order to be manifest, and that it can be attained perhaps more certainly without waiting for words and without even taking them into account, in a thousand external signs, even in certain invisible phenomena, analogous in the world of characters to what atmospheric changes are in the world of physical nature."[1]

Diverse, too, are the things, enterprises, and values to which intelligence tends. It impels us to *conversation*, in which we exchange and communicate ideas. It incites us to *friendship*, based on the community of ideas and sentiments. It invites us to *philosophy*, a voluntary and premeditated exercise of thought by which we may determine the order and content of objective significations. Let us retain the essential point that friendship and philosophy are subject to the same criticism. According to Proust, friends are like well-disposed minds that are explicitly in agreement as to the signification of things, words, and ideas; but the philosopher too is a thinker who presupposes in himself the benevolence of thought, who attributes to thought the natural love of truth and to truth the explicit determination of what is naturally worked out by thought. This is why Proust sets in opposition to the traditional pairing of friendship and philosophy a more obscure pairing formed by love and art. A mediocre love is worth more than a great friendship because love is rich in signs and is fed by silent interpretation. A work of art is worth more than a philosophical work; for what is enveloped in the sign is more profound than all the explicit significations. What does violence to us is richer than all the fruits of our goodwill or of our conscious work, and more important than thought is "what is food for thought" (II, 549). In all its forms, intelligence attains by itself, and makes us attain, only those abstract and conventional truths that have merely a *possible* value. What is the worth of these objective truths that result from a combination of work, intelligence, and goodwill but are communicated to the degree that they occur, and occur to the degree that they may be received? Concerning an intonation of Berma's, Proust says: "It was because of its very clarity that it did not satisfy me. The intonation was ingenious, of an intention and meaning so defined that it seemed to exist in and of itself, as if any intelligent artist might have acquired it" (I, 567).

At the outset, the hero of the Search participates more or less in all the objective beliefs. More precisely, the fact that he participates less in the illusion within a certain realm of signs, or that he rapidly frees himself from it at a certain level, does not prevent the illusion from persisting on another level, in another realm. Thus it does not seem that the hero has ever had a great talent for friendship; to him friendship has always seemed secondary, and a friend more valuable in terms of the spectacle he affords than by a community of the ideas or sentiments he might inspire. "Superior men" teach him nothing: even Bergotte or Elstir cannot communicate to him any truth that could spare him from serving his personal apprenticeship and from passing through the signs and disappointments to which he is doomed. Very soon, then, he realizes that a superior mind or even a great friend are worth no more than even a brief love. But it so happens that in love it is already more difficult for him to rid himself of the corresponding objectivist illusion. It is his collective love for the young girls, the slow individualization of Albertine, and the accidents of choice that teach him that the reasons for loving never inhere in the person loved but refer to ghosts, to Third Parties, to Themes that are incarnated in himself according to complex laws. He learns thereby that avowal is not essential to love and that it is neither necessary nor desirable to declare himself: we shall be lost, all our freedom lost, if we give the object the benefit of the signs and significations that transcend it. "Since the time of our games in the Champs-Elysées, my conception of love had changed, if the beings to whom my love was successively attached remained virtually identical. On the one hand, the avowal, the declaration of my feelings to the woman I loved, no longer seemed to me one of the crucial and necessary scenes of love nor love itself an external reality..." (I, 925).

How difficult it is, in each realm, to renounce this belief in an external reality. The sensuous signs lay a trap for us and invite us to seek their meaning in the object that bears or emits them, so that the possibility of failure, the abandonment of interpretation, is like the worm in the fruit. And even once we have conquered the objectivist illusions in most realms, they still subsist in Art, where we continue to believe that we should be able to listen, look, describe, address ourselves to the object, to decompose and analyze it in order to extract a truth from it.

The hero of the Search, however, realizes the defects of an objectivist literature. He often insists on his impotence to observe or to describe. Proust's hatreds are famous: of Sainte-Beuve, for whom the discovery of truth is inseparable from a *causerie*, a conversational method by which truth is to be extracted from the most arbitrary data, starting with the confidences of those who claim to have known someone well; of the Goncourts, who decompose a character or an object, turn it around, analyze its architecture, retrace its outlines and projections in order to discover exotic truths in them (the Goncourts too believed in the prestige of conversation); of realistic and popular art that credits intelligible values, well-defined significations, major subjects. Methods must be judged according to their results: for example, the wretched things Sainte-Beuve writes on Balzac, Stendhal, or Baudelaire. *And what could the Goncourts understand about the Verdurin circle, about Cottard?* Nothing, judging by the pastiche in the Search; they report and analyze what is *intentionally* spoken, but miss the most obvious signs—the sign of Cottard's stupidity, the grotesque gestures and symbols of Mme Verdurin. And the characteristic of popular and proletarian art is that it takes the workers for fools. A literature is disappointing if it interprets signs by referring them to objects that can be designated (observation and description), if it surrounds itself with pseudo-objective guarantees of evidence and communication (*causerie*, investigation), and if it confuses meaning with intelligible, explicit, and formulated signification (major subjects).[2] The hero of the Search always feels alien to this conception of art and literature. But then, why does he suffer so intense a disappointment each time he realizes its inanity? Because art, at least, found in this conception a specific fulfillment: it espoused life in order to exalt it, in order to disengage its value and truth. And when we protest against an art of observation and description, how do we know if it is not our incapacity to observe, to describe, that inspires this protest, and our incapacity to understand life? We think we are reacting against an illusory form of art, but perhaps we are reacting against an infirmity of our own nature, against a lack of the will-to-live—so that our disappointment is not simply the kind afforded by an objective literature, but also the kind afforded by our incapacity to succeed in this form of literature (III, 720–23). Despite his repugnance, then, the hero of the Search cannot keep from dreaming of gifts of observation that might over-come, in him, the intermittences of inspiration: "but in giving myself this consolation of a possible human observation that would replace an impossible inspiration, I knew I was merely trying to give myself a consolation..." (III, 855). The disappointment of literature is thus insepara-bly double: "Literature could no longer afford me any joy, *either* by my own fault, being insufficiently gifted, *or* by literature's fault, if it was indeed less charged with reality than I had believed" (III, 862).

Disappointment is a fundamental moment of the search or of apprenticeship: in each realm of signs, we are disappointed when the object does not give us the secret we were expecting. And disappointment itself is pluralist, variable according to each line. There are few things that are not disappointing the first time they are seen. For the first time is the time of inexperience; we are not yet ca-pable of distinguishing the sign from the object, and the object interposes and confuses the signs. Disappointment on first hearing Vinteuil, on first meeting Bergotte, on first seeing the Balbec church. And it is not enough to return to things a second time, for voluntary memory and this very return offer disadvantages analogous to those that kept us the first time from freely enjoying the signs (the second stay at Balbec is no less disappointing than the first, from other aspects).

How is this disappointment, in each realm, to be reme-died? On each line of apprenticeship, the hero undergoes an analogous experience, at various moments: *for the dis-appointment of the object, he attempts to find a subjective com-pensation.* When he sees, then comes to know Mme de

Guermantes, he realizes that she does not contain the secret of her name's meaning. Her face and body are not colored by the hue of the syllables. What is to be done except to compensate for the disappointment? To become personally sensitive to less profound signs that are yet more appropriate to the Duchess's charm, as a result of the association of ideas that she stimulates in us. "That Mme de Guermantes was like the others had been a disappointment for me at first; it was now, in reaction, and with the help of so many good wines, an astonishment" (II, 524).

The mechanism of objective disappointment and of subjective compensation is specially analyzed in the example of the theater. The hero passionately longs to hear Berma, but when he does, he tries first of all to recognize her talent, to encircle this talent, to isolate it in order to be able to designate it. It is Berma, "at last I am seeing Berma." He notices a particularly intelligent intonation, admirably placed. All at once it is Phèdre, it is Phèdre in person. Yet nothing can prevent the disappointment: for this intonation has only an intelligible value, it is only the fruit of intelligence and work (I, 567). Perhaps it was necessary to listen to Berma differently. Those signs we had not been able to relish or to interpret so long as we linked them to Berma's person — perhaps their meaning was to be sought elsewhere: in associations that were neither in Phèdre nor in Berma. Thus Bergotte teaches the hero that a certain gesture of Berma's evokes that of an archaic statuette the actress could never have seen, but which Racine himself had certainly never thought of either (I, 560).

Each line of apprenticeship undergoes these two moments: the disappointment afforded by an attempted objective interpretation, then the attempted remedy of this disappointment by a subjective interpretation in which we reconstruct associative series. This is the case in love and even in art. We may easily understand the reason. It is because the sign is doubtless more profound than the object emitting it, but it is still attached to that object, it is still half sheathed in it. And the sign's meaning is doubtless more profound than the subject interpreting it, but it is attached to this subject, half incarnated in a series of subjective associations. We proceed from one to the other; we leap from one to the other; we overcome the disappointment of the object by a compensation of the subject.

Thus we shall scarcely be surprised to realize that the moment of compensation remains in itself inadequate and does not provide a definitive revelation. For objective, intelligible values we substitute a subjective association of ideas. The inadequacy of this compensation appears all the more clearly the higher we mount on the ladder of signs. A gesture of Berma's is beautiful because it evokes that of a statuette. But also Vinteuil's music is beautiful because it evokes for us a walk in the Bois de Boulogne (I, 533). Everything is permitted in the exercise of associations. From this viewpoint, we shall find no difference of nature between the pleasure of art and that of the madeleine: everywhere, the procession of past contiguities. Doubtless even the experience of the madeleine is not truly reduced to simple associations of ideas, but we are not yet in a position to understand why, and, in reducing the quality of a work of art to the flavor of the madeleine, we deprive ourselves forever of the means of understanding it. Far from leading us to a true appreciation of art, subjective compensation ends by making the work of art itself into a mere link in our associations of ideas: as in the case of Swann who never admires Giotto or Botticelli so much as when he discovers their style in the face of a kitchen maid or of a beloved woman. Or else we construct our own private museum, in which the flavor of a madeleine, the quality of a draft of air prevail over any beauty: "I was indifferent to the beauties they showed me and was thrilled by vague reminiscences. . . . I stood in an ecstasy, sniffing the odor of a draft through the open door. Apparently you have a predilection for drafts, they told me" (II, 944).

Yet what else is there except the object and the subject? The example of Berma tells us. The hero of the Search will finally understand that neither Berma nor Phèdre are designable characters, nor are they elements of association. Phèdre is a *role*, and Berma unites herself with this role — not in the sense in which the role would still be an object or something subjective — on the contrary, it is a world, a spiritual milieu populated by essences. Berma, bearer of signs, renders them so immaterial that they grant access to these essences and are filled by them. So that even in a mediocre role, Berma's gestures still reveal to us a world of possible essences (II, 47–51).

Beyond designated objects, beyond intelligible and formulated truths, but also beyond subjective chains of association and resurrections by resemblance or contiguity, are the essences that are alogical or supralogical. They transcend the states of subjectivity no less than the properties of the object. It is the essence that constitutes the sign insofar as it is irreducible to the object emitting it; it is the essence that constitutes the meaning insofar as it is irreducible to the subject apprehending it. It is the essence that is the last word of the apprenticeship or the final revelation. Now, more than by Berma, it is by the work of art, by painting and music and especially by the problem of literature, that the hero of the Search arrives at this revelation of essences. The worldly signs, the signs of love, even the sensuous signs are incapable of giving us the essence; they bring us closer to it, but we always fall back into the trap of the object, into the snare of subjectivity. It is only on the level of art that the essences are revealed. But *once* they are manifested in the work of art, they react upon all the other realms; we learn that they *already* incarnated, that they were already there in all these kinds of signs, in all the types of apprenticeship.

CHAPTER 4

Essences and the Signs of Art

What is the superiority of the signs of art over all the others? It is that the others are material. Material, first of all, by their emission: they are half sheathed in the object bearing them. Sensuous qualities, loved faces are still matter. (It is no accident that the significant sensuous qualities are above all odors and flavors: the most material of qualities.) *Only the signs of art are immaterial.* Of course Vinteuil's little phrase is uttered by the piano and the violin. Of course it can be decomposed materially: five notes very close together, two of which recur. But in their case, as in Plato, 3 + 2 explains nothing. The piano here is merely the spatial image of an entirely different keyboard; the notes merely the "sonorous appearance" of an entirely spiritual entity. "As if the performers not so much played the little phrase as executed the rites necessary for it to appear..." (I, 347). In this regard, the very impression of the little phrase is *sine materia* (I, 209).

Berma, too, uses her voice, her arms. But her gestures, instead of testifying to "muscular connections," form a transparent body that refracts an essence, an Idea. Mediocre actresses must weep in order to signify grief. "Redundant tears visibly shed because the actress had not been able to internalize them, over the marble voice of Ismene or Aricie." But all of Berma's expressions, as in the performance of a great violinist, have become qualities of timbre. In her voice "subsisted not one scrap of inert matter refractory to spirit" (II, 48).

The other signs are material not only by their origin and by the way they remain half sheathed in the object, but also by their development or their "explication." The madeleine refers us to Combray, the cobblestones to Venice, and so on. Doubtless the two impressions, the present one and the past, have one and the same quality, but they are no less materially two. So that each time memory intervenes, the explanation of the signs still involves something material (III, 375). The steeples of Martinville, in the order of sensuous signs, already constitute a less "material" example because they appeal to desire and to imagination, not to memory (III, 375). Still the impression of the steeple is explained by the image of three young girls; in order to be the girls of our imagination, these latter in their turn are no less materially different than the steeples.

Proust often speaks of the necessity that weighs upon him: that something always reminds him of or makes him imagine something else. But whatever the importance of this process of analogy in art, art does not find its profoundest formula here. As long as we discover a sign's meaning in something else, matter still subsists, refractory to spirit. On the contrary, art gives us the true unity: unity of an immaterial sign and of an entirely spiritual meaning. The essence is precisely this unity of sign and meaning as it is revealed in the work of art. Essences or Ideas, that is what each sign of the little phrase reveals (I, 349). That is what gives the phrase its real existence, independent of the instruments and the sounds that reproduce or incarnate it more than they compose it. The superiority of art over life consists in this: all the signs we meet in life are still material signs, and their meaning, because it is always in something else, is not altogether spiritual.

What is an essence as revealed in the work of art? It is a difference, the absolute and ultimate Difference. Difference is what constitutes being, what makes us conceive being. This is why art, insofar as it manifests essences, is alone capable of giving us what we sought in vain from life: "The diversity that I had vainly sought from life, from travel..." (III, 159). "The world of difference not existing on the surface of the Earth, among all the countries our perception standardizes, does not exist with all the more reason in what we call *the world*. Does it exist, moreover, anywhere? Vinteuil's septet had seemed to tell me so" (III, 277).

But what is an absolute, ultimate difference? Not an empirical difference between two things or two objects, always extrinsic. Proust gives a first approximation of essence when he says it is something in a subject, something like the presence of a final quality at the heart of a subject: an internal difference, "*a qualitative difference* that there is in the way the world looks to us, a difference that, if there were no such thing as art, would remain the eternal secret of each man" (III, 895). In this regard, Proust is Leibnizian: the essences are veritable monads, each defined by the viewpoint to which it expresses the world, each viewpoint itself referring to an ultimate quality at the heart of the monad. As Leibniz says, they have neither doors nor windows: the viewpoint being the difference itself, viewpoints toward a world supposedly the same are as different as the most remote worlds. This is why friendship never establishes anything but false communications, based on misunderstandings, and frames only false windows. This is why love, more lucid, makes it a principle to renounce all communication. Our only windows, our only doors are entirely spiritual; there is no intersubjectivity except an artistic one. Only art gives us what we vainly sought from a friend, what we would have vainly expected from the beloved. "Only by art can we emerge from ourselves, can we know what another sees of this universe that is not the same as ours and whose landscapes would have remained as unknown to us as those that might be on the moon. Thanks to art, instead of seeing a single world, our own, we see it multiply, and as many original artists as there are, so many worlds will we have at our disposal, more different from each other than those that circle in the void . . ." (III, 895–96).

Are we to conclude from this that essence is subjective, and that the difference is between subjects rather than between objects? This would be to overlook the texts in which Proust treats the essences as Platonic Ideas and confers upon them an independent reality. Even Vinteuil has "revealed" the phrase more than he has created it (I, 349–51).

Each subject expresses the world from a certain viewpoint. But the viewpoint is the difference itself, the absolute internal difference. Each subject therefore expresses an absolutely different world. And doubtless the world so expressed does not exist outside the subject expressing it (what we call the external world is only the disappointing projection, the standardizing limit of all these worlds expressed). But the world expressed is not identified with the subject; it is distinguished from the subject precisely as essence is distinguished from existence, even from the subject's own existence. Essence does not exist outside the subject expressing it, but it is expressed as the essence not of the subject but of Being, or of the region of Being that is revealed to the subject. This is why each essence is a *patrie*, a country (III, 257). It is not reducible to a psychological state, nor to a psychological subjectivity, nor even to some form of a higher subjectivity. Essence is indeed the final quality at the heart of a subject; but this quality is deeper than the subject, of a different order: "Unknown quality of a unique world" (III, 376). It is not the subject that explains essence, rather it is essence that implicates, envelops, wraps itself up in the subject. Rather, in coiling round itself, it is essence that constitutes subjectivity. It is not the individuals who constitute the world, but the worlds enveloped, the essences that constitute the individuals. "These worlds that we call individuals, and which without art we would never know" (III, 258). Essence is not only individual, it *individualizes*.

The viewpoint is not identified with the person who assumes it; the internal quality is not identified with the subject it individualizes. This distinction between essence and subject is all the more important in that Proust sees it as the only possible proof of the soul's immortality. In the soul of the person who reveals or merely understands the essence, it is a kind of "divine captive" (I, 350). Essences, perhaps, have imprisoned themselves, have enveloped themselves in these souls they individualize. They exist only in such captivity, but they are not to be separated from the "unknown country" in which they envelop themselves inside us. They are our "hostages": they die if we die, but if they are eternal, we are immortal in some fashion. They therefore make death less likely; the only proof, the only hope, is aesthetic. Hence two questions are fundamentally linked: "The question of the reality of Art, the question of the reality of the soul's Eternity" (III, 374). Bergotte's death in front of Vermeer's little patch of yellow wall becomes symbolic in this regard: "In a celestial scale there appeared to him, weighing down one of its trays, his own life, while the other tray contained the little patch of yellow wall so beautifully painted. He felt that he had unwisely given the first for the second. . . . He suffered another stroke. . . . He was dead. Dead forever? Who can say?" (III, 187).

The world enveloped by essence is always a beginning of the World in general, a beginning of the universe, an absolute, radical beginning. "At first the piano alone complained, like a bird abandoned in its countryside; the violin heard, replied from a neighboring tree. It was like the beginning of the world, as if there had been, as yet, only the two of them on Earth, or rather in this world closed to all the rest, constructed by the logic of a creator in such a way that only the two of them would ever exist: this sonata" (I, 352). What Proust says of the sea, or even of a girl's face, is much more true of essences and of the work of art: the unstable opposition, "this perpetual recreation of the primordial elements of nature" (I, 906). But so defined, essence is the birth of Time itself. Not that time is already deployed: it does not yet have the distinct dimensions according to which it can unfold, nor even the separate series in which it is distributed according to different rhythms. Certain Neoplatonists used a profound word to designate the original state that precedes any development, any deployment, any "explication": *complication*, which envelops the many in the One and affirms the unity of the multiple. Eternity did not seem to them the absence of change, nor even the extension of a limitless existence, but the complicated state of time itself (*uno ictu mutationes tuas complectitur*). The Word, *omnia complicans*, and containing all essences, was defined as the supreme complication, the complication of contraries, the unstable opposition. From this they derived the notion of an essentially expressive universe, organized according to degrees of immanent complications and following an order of descending explications.

The least we can say is that Charlus is complicated. But the word must be taken in its full etymological sense. Charlus's genius is to retain all the souls that compose him in the "complicated" state: this is how it happens that Charlus always has the freshness of a world just created and unceasingly emits primordial signs that the interpreter must decipher, that is, explicate.

Nonetheless, if we look for something in life that corresponds to the situation of the original essences, we shall not find it in this or that character, but rather in a certain profound state. This state is sleep. The sleeper "holds in a circle around him the thread of hours, the order of years and worlds": wonderful freedom that ceases only upon awakening, when he is constrained to choose according to the order of time redeployed (I, 4–5). Similarly, the artist-subject has the revelation of an original time, coiled, complicated within essence itself, embracing simultaneously all its series and dimensions. Here is the true sense of the expression "time regained," which is understood in the signs of art. It is not to be confused with another kind of time regained, that of the sensuous signs. The time of sensuous signs is only a time regained at the heart of lost time; hence it mobilizes all the resources of involuntary memory and gives us a simple image of eternity. But, like sleep, art is beyond memory; it appeals to pure thought as a faculty of essences. What art regains for us is time as it is coiled within essence, as it is born in the world enveloped by essence, identical to eternity. Proust's extratemporality is this time in a nascent state, and the artist-subject who regains it. This is why, in all strictness, there is only the work of art that lets us regain time: the work of art is "the only means of regaining time lost" (III, 899). It bears the highest signs, whose meaning is situated in a primordial complication, a veritable eternity, an absolute original time.

But precisely how is essence incarnated in the work of art? Or, what comes down to the same thing, how does an artist-subject manage to "communicate" the essence that individualizes him and makes him eternal? It is incarnated in substances. But these substances are ductile, so kneaded and refined that they become entirely spiritual; they are of course color for the painter, like Vermeer's yellow, sound for the musician, words for the writer. But, more profoundly, they are free substances that are expressed equally well through words, sounds, and colors. For example, in Thomas Hardy, the blocks of stone, the geometry of these blocks, and the parallelism of their lines form a spiritualized substance from which the words themselves derive their arrangement; in Stendhal, altitude is an aerial substance, "linked to spiritual life" (III, 377). The real theme of a work is therefore not the subject the words designate, but the unconscious themes, the involuntary archetypes in which the words, but also the colors and the sounds, assume their meaning and their life. Art is a veritable transmutation of substance. By it, substance is spiritualized and physical surroundings dematerialized in order to refract essence, that is, the quality of an original world. This treatment of substance is indissociable from "style."

As the quality of a world, essence is never to be confused with an object but on the contrary brings together two quite different objects, concerning which we in fact perceive that they have this quality in the revealing medium. At the same time that essence is incarnated in a substance, the ultimate quality constituting it is therefore expressed as the *quality common* to two different objects, kneaded in this luminous substance, plunged into this refracting medium. It is in this that style consists: "One can string out in indefinite succession, in a description, the objects that figured in the described place; the truth will begin only when the writer takes two different objects, posits their relation, analogous in the world of art to that of the causal law in the world of science, and envelops them in the necessary rings of a great style" (III, 889). Which is to say that style is essentially metaphor. But metaphor is essentially metamorphosis and indicates how the two objects exchange their determinations, exchange even the names that designate them, in the new medium that confers the common quality upon them. Thus in Elstir's painting, where the sea becomes land, the land sea, where the city is designated only by "marine terms" and the water by "urban terms" (I, 835–37). This is because style, in order to spiritualize substance and render it adequate to essence, reproduces the unstable opposition, the original complication, the struggle and exchange of the primordial elements that constitute essence itself. In Vinteuil's music we hear two motifs struggling, as if in bodily combat: "combat of energies alone, actually, for if these beings confronted each other, it was to be rid of their physical bodies, their appearance, their name..." (III, 260). An essence is always a birth of the world, but style is that continuous and refracted birth, that birth regained in substances adequate to essences, that birth which has become the metamorphosis of objects. Style is not the man, style is essence itself.

Essence is not only particular, not only individual, but is individualizing. Essence individualizes and determines the substances in which it is incarnated, like the objects it encloses within the rings of style, thus Vinteuil's reddening septet and white sonata or the splendid diversity within Wagner's work (III, 159). This is because essence is in itself difference. But it does not have the power to diversify, and to diversify itself, without also having the power to repeat itself, identical to itself. What can one do with essence, which is ultimate difference, except to repeat it, because it is irreplaceable and because nothing can be substituted for it? This is why great music can only be played again, a poem learned by heart and recited. Difference and repetition are only apparently in opposition. There is no great artist who does not make us say: "The same and yet different" (III, 259).

This is because difference, as the quality of a world, is affirmed only through a kind of autorepetition that traverses the various media and reunites different objects; repetition constitutes the degrees of an original difference, but diversity also constitutes the levels of a repetition no less fundamental. About the work of a great artist, we say: it's the same thing, on a different level. But we also say: it's different, but to the same degree. Actually, difference and repetition are the two inseparable and correlative powers of essence. An artist does not "age" because he repeats himself, for repetition is the power of difference, no less than difference the power of repetition. An artist "ages" when, "by exhaustion of his brain," he decides it is simpler to find directly in life, as though ready-made, what he can express only in his work, what he should have distinguished and repeated by means of his work (I, 852). The aging artist puts his trust in life, in the "beauty of life," but he gets no more than substitutes for what constitutes art, repetitions that have become mechanical because they are external, frozen differences that revert to a substance that they can no longer make light and spiritual. Life does not have the two powers of art; it receives them only by corrupting them and reproduces essence only on the lowest level, to the weakest degree.

Art therefore has an absolute privilege, which is expressed in several ways. In art, substances are spiritualized, media dematerialized. The work of art is therefore a world of signs, but they are immaterial and no longer have anything opaque about them, at least to the artist's eye, the artist's ear. In the second place, the meaning of these signs is an essence, an essence affirmed in all its power. In the third place, sign and meaning, essence and transmuted substance, are identified or united in a perfect adequation. Identity of a sign as style and of a meaning as essence: such is the character of the work of art. And doubtless art itself has been the object of an apprenticeship. We have undergone the objectivist temptation, the subjectivist compensation as in every other realm. The fact remains that the revelation of essence (beyond the object, beyond the subject himself) belongs only to the realm of art. If it is to occur, it will occur there. This is why art is the finality of the world, and the apprentice's unconscious destination.

We then find ourselves facing two kinds of questions. What is the worth of the other signs, those that constitute the realms of life? In and of themselves, what do they teach us? Can we say that they already set us on the path of art, and how? But above all, once we have received from art the final revelation, how will this revelation react on the other realms and become the center of a system that leaves nothing outside itself? Essence is always an artistic essence. But once discovered, it is incarnated not only in spiritualized substances, in the immaterial signs of the work of art, but also in other realms, which will henceforth be integrated into the work of art. It passes then into media that are more opaque, into signs that are more material. It loses there certain of its original characteristics, assumes others that express the descent of essence into these increasingly rebellious substances. There are laws of the transformation of essence in relation to the determinations of life.

CHAPTER 5

The Secondary Role of Memory

The worldly signs and the signs of love, in order to be interpreted, appeal to the intelligence. It is the intelligence that deciphers: on condition that it "comes after," obliged to function under the pressure of that nervous exaltation that worldliness affords or that pain that love inspires. Doubtless intelligence mobilizes other faculties as well. We see the jealous man employing all the resources of memory in order to interpret the signs of love—the beloved's lies. But memory, not solicited directly here, can furnish only a voluntary aid. And precisely because it is only "voluntary," memory always comes too late in relation to the signs to be deciphered. The jealous man's memory tries to retain everything because the slightest detail may turn out to be a sign or a symptom of deception, so that the intelligence will have the material requisite to its forthcoming interpretations. Hence there is something sublime in the jealous man's memory; it confronts its own limits and, straining toward the future, seeks to transcend them. But it comes too late, for it cannot distinguish within the moment that phrase that should be retained, that gesture that it could not yet know would assume a certain meaning (III, 61). "Later, confronting the lie in so many words or seized by an anxious doubt, I would try to remember; it was no use, my memory had not been forewarned in time, it had decided there was no use keeping a copy" (III, 153). In short, memory intervenes in the interpretations of the signs of love only in a voluntary form that dooms it to a pathetic failure. It is not the effort of memory, as it appears in each love, which succeeds in deciphering the corresponding signs; it is only the pressure of the intelligence, in the series of successive loves, characterized over and over again by forgetting and by unconscious repetitions.

At what level, then, does the famous *involuntary* Memory intervene? It will be noticed that it intervenes only in terms of a sign of a very special type: the sensuous signs. We apprehend a sensuous quality as a sign; we feel an imperative that forces us to seek its meaning. Then it happens that involuntary Memory, directly solicited by the sign, yields us this meaning (thus Combray for the madeleine, Venice for the cobblestones, and so forth).

We notice, secondly, that this involuntary memory does not possess the secret of all the sensuous signs: some refer to desire and to figures of the imagination (for instance the steeples of Martinville). This is why Proust carefully distinguishes two cases of sensuous signs: reminiscences and discoveries — the "resurrections of memory," and the "truths written with the help of figures" (III, 879). In the morning, when the hero gets up, he experiences within himself not only the pressure of involuntary memories that are identified with a light or an odor, but also the energy of involuntary desires that are incarnated in a woman passing by — a laundress or a proud young lady, "an image, at least..." (III, 27). At the beginning, we cannot even say where the sign comes from. Does the sensuous quality address the imagination or simply the memory? We must try everything, in order to discover the faculty that will yield us the adequate meaning. And when we fail, we cannot know whether the meaning that remains veiled was a dream figure or a buried recollection of involuntary memory. The three trees, for example: were they a landscape of Memory or a Dream? (I, 718-19).

The sensuous signs that are explained by involuntary memory have a double inferiority, not only in relation to the signs of art, but even in relation to the sensuous signs that refer to the imagination. On the one hand their substance is more opaque and refractory, their explication remains too material. On the other hand they only apparently surmount the contradiction of being and nothingness (as we have seen, in the hero's recollection of his grandmother). Proust speaks of the fulfillment of reminiscences or of involuntary recollections, of the supreme joys afforded by the signs of Memory and of the time they suddenly allow us to recapture. It is true: the sensuous signs that are explained by memory form a "beginning of art;" they set us "on the path of art" (III, 889). Our apprenticeship would never find its realization in art if it did not pass through those signs that give us a foretaste of time regained, and prepare us for the fulfillment of aesthetic Ideas. But they do nothing more than prepare us: a mere beginning. They are still signs of life and not signs of art itself.[1]

They are superior to the worldly signs, superior to the signs of love, but inferior to those of art. And, even of their own kind, they are inferior to the sensuous signs of the imagination, that are closer to art (though still belonging to life) (III, 375). Proust often presents the signs of memory as decisive; reminiscences seem to him constitutive of the work of art, not only in the perspective of his personal project, but in the great precursors, in Chateaubriand, Nerval, or Baudelaire. But, if reminiscences are integrated into art as constitutive elements, it is rather to the degree that they are conducting elements that lead the reader to the comprehension of the work, the artist to the conception of his task and of the unity of that task: "That it was precisely and solely this kind of sensation that must *lead* to the work of art was what I would try conclusively to prove" (III, 918). Reminiscences are metaphors of life; metaphors are reminiscences of art. Both, in effect, have something in common: they determine a relation between two entirely different objects "in order to withdraw them from the contingencies of time" (III, 889). But art alone succeeds entirely in what life has merely sketched out. Reminiscences in involuntary memory are still of life: of art at the level of life, hence bad metaphors. On the contrary, art in its essence, the art superior to life, is not based upon involuntary memory. It is not even based upon imagination and unconscious figures. The signs of art are explained by pure thought as a faculty of essences. Of the sensuous signs in general, whether they are addressed to the memory or even to the imagination, we must say sometimes that they precede art and that they merely lead us to art, sometimes that they succeed art and that they merely gather its nearest reflections.

How to explain the complex mechanism of reminiscences? At first sight, it is an associative mechanism: on the one hand, a resemblance between a present and a past sensation; on the other hand, a contiguity of the past sensation with a whole that we experienced then and that revives under the effect of the present sensation. Thus the flavor of the madeleine is like that which we tasted at Combray, and it revives Combray, where we tasted it for the first time. The formal importance of an associationist psychology in Proust has often been noted. But it would be a mistake to reproach him for this: associationism is less outmoded than the critique of associationism. We must therefore ask from what viewpoint the cases of reminiscence effectively transcend the mechanisms of association and also from what viewpoint they effectively refer to such mechanisms.

Reminiscence raises several problems that are not solved by the association of ideas. First, what is the source of the extraordinary joy that we already feel in the present sensation? A joy so powerful that it suffices to make us indifferent to death. Second, how to explain the absence of any simple resemblance between the two sensations, present and past? Beyond a resemblance, we discover between two sensations the identity of a quality in one and the other. Finally, how to explain that Combray rises up, not as it was experienced in contiguity with the past sensation, but in a splendor, with a "truth" that never had an equivalent in reality?

This joy of time regained, this identity of the sensuous quality, this truth of the reminiscence—we experience them, and we feel that they overflow all the associative mechanisms. But we are unable to say how. We acknowledge what is happening, but we do not yet possess the means of understanding it. With the flavor of the madeleine, Combray has risen up in all its splendor; but we have by no means discovered the causes of such an apparition. The impression of the three trees remains unexplained; on the contrary, the impression of the madeleine seems explained by Combray. Yet we are scarcely any further along: why this joy, why this splendor in the resurrection of Combray? ("I had then postponed seeking the profound causes" [III, 867].)

Voluntary memory proceeds from an actual present to a present that "has been," to something that was present and is so no longer. The past of voluntary memory is therefore doubly relative: relative to the present that it has been, but also to the present with regard to which it is now past. That is, this memory does not apprehend the past directly; it recomposes it with different *presents*. This is why Proust makes the same criticism of voluntary memory as of conscious perception; the latter claims it finds the secret of the impression in the object, the former claims it finds the secret of memory in the succession of presents. Precisely — it is objects that distinguish the successive presents. Voluntary memory proceeds by snapshots (*instantanés*): "The word itself made it as boring to me as an exhibition of photographs, and I felt no more taste, no more talent, for describing now what I had once seen, than yesterday what I had observed with a scrupulous and gloomy eye at that very moment" (III, 865).

It is obvious that something essential escapes voluntary memory: the past's being *as past*. Voluntary memory proceeds as if the past were constituted as such after it has been present. It would therefore have to wait for a new present so that the preceding one could pass by, or become past. But in this way the essence of time escapes us. For if the present was not past at the same time as present, if the same moment did not coexist with itself as present *and* past, it would never pass, a new present would never come to replace this one. The past as it is in itself coexists with, and does not succeed, the present it has been. It is true that we do not apprehend something as past at the very moment when we experience it as present (except in cases of paramnesia, which may account for the vision, in Proust, of the three trees) (I, 718–19). But this is because the joint demands of conscious perception and of voluntary memory establish a real succession where, more profoundly, there is a virtual coexistence.

If there is a resemblance between Bergson's conceptions and Proust's, it is on this level — not on the level of duration, but of memory. That we do not proceed from an actual present to the past, that we do not recompose the past with various presents, but that we place ourselves, directly, in the past itself. That this past does not represent something that has been, but simply something that is and that coexists with itself as present. That the past does not have to preserve itself in anything but itself, because it is in itself, survives and preserves itself in itself — such are the famous theses of *Matter and Memory*. This being of the past in itself is what Bergson called the virtual. Similarly Proust, when he speaks of states induced by the signs of memory: "Real without being present, ideal without being abstract" (II, 873). It is true that, starting from this point, the problem is not the same in Proust as in Bergson: it is enough for Bergson to know that the past is preserved in itself. Despite his profound pages on dreams or on paramnesia, Bergson does not ask essentially how the past, as it is in itself, could also be saved for us. Even the deepest dream implies, according to Bergson, a corruption of pure memory, a descent from memory into an image that distorts it. While Proust's problem is, indeed: how to save for ourselves the past as it is preserved in itself, as it survives in itself? Proust manages to set forth the Bergsonian thesis, not directly, but according to an anecdote "of the Norwegian philosopher" who has heard it himself from Boutroux (II, 983–85). Let us note Proust's reaction: "We all possess our memories, if not the faculty of recalling them, the great Norwegian philosopher says according to M. Bergson.... But what is a memory that one does not recall?" Proust asks the question: how shall we save the past as it is in itself? It is to this question that involuntary Memory offers its answer.

Involuntary memory seems to be based first of all upon the resemblance between two sensations, between two moments. But, more profoundly, the resemblance refers us to a strict *identity* of a quality common to the two sensations or of a sensation common to the two moments, the present and the past. Thus the flavor: it seems that it contains a volume of duration that extends it through two moments at once. But, in its turn, the sensation, the identical quality, implies a relation with something *different*. The flavor of the madeleine has, in its volume, imprisoned and enveloped Combray. So long as we remain on the level of conscious perception, the madeleine has only an entirely external relation of contiguity with Combray. So long as we remain on the level of voluntary memory, Combray remains external to the madeleine, as the separable context of the past sensation. But this is the characteristic of involuntary memory: it internalizes the context, it makes the past context inseparable from the present sensation. At the same time that the resemblance between the two moments is transcended in the direction of a more profound identity, the contiguity that belonged to the past moment is transcended in the direction of a more profound difference. Combray rises up again in the present sensation in which its difference from the past sensation is internalized. The present sensation is therefore no longer separable from this relation with the different object. *The essential thing in involuntary memory is not resemblance, nor even identity, which are merely conditions, but the internalized difference, which becomes immanent.* It is in this sense that reminiscence is the analogue of art, and involuntary memory the analogue of a metaphor: it takes "two different objects," the madeleine with its flavor, Combray with its qualities of color and temperature; it envelops the one in the other, and makes their relation into something internal.

Flavor, the quality common to the two sensations, the sensation common to the two moments, is here only to recall something else: Combray. But upon this invocation, Combray rises up in a form that is absolutely new. Combray does not rise up as it was once present; Combray rises up as past, but this past is no longer relative to the present that it has been, it is no longer relative to the present in relation to which it is now past. This is no longer the Combray of perception nor of voluntary memory. Combray appears as it could not be experienced: not in reality, but in its truth; not in its external and contingent relations, but in its internalized difference, in its essence. Combray rises up in a pure past, coexisting with the two presents, but out of their reach, out of reach of the present voluntary memory and of the past conscious perception. "A morsel of time in the pure state" (III, 872) is not a simple resemblance between the present and the past, between a present that is immediate and a past that has been present, not even an identity in the two moments, but beyond, *the very being of the past in itself*, deeper than any past that has been, than any present that was. "A morsel of time, in the pure state," that is, the localized essence of time.

"Real without being present, ideal without being abstract." This ideal reality, this virtuality, is essence, which is realized or incarnated in involuntary memory. Here as in art, envelopment or involution remains the superior state of essence. And involuntary memory retains its two powers: the difference in the past moment, the repetition in the present one. But essence is realized in involuntary memory to a lesser degree than in art; it is incarnated in a more opaque matter. First of all, essence no longer appears as the ultimate quality of a singular viewpoint, as did artistic essence, which was individual and even individualizing. Doubtless it is particular, but it is a principle of localization rather than of individuation. It appears as a local essence: Combray, Balbec, Venice. It is also particular because it reveals the differential truth of a place, of a moment. But, from another viewpoint, it is already general because it grants this revelation in a sensation "common" to two places, to two moments. In art, too, the quality of essence was expressed as a quality common to two objects, but the artistic essence thereby lost nothing of its singularity, was not alienated, because the two objects and their relation were entirely determined by the point of view of essence, without any margin of contingence. This is no longer the case with regard to involuntary memory: essence begins to assume a minimum of generality. This is why Proust says that the sensuous signs already refer to a "general essence," like the signs of love or the worldly signs (III, 918).

A second difference appears from the viewpoint of time. The artistic essence reveals an original time, which surmounts its series and its dimensions. This is a time "complicated" within essence itself, identical to eternity. Hence, when we speak of "time regained" in the work of art, we are concerned with that primordial time that is in opposition to time deployed and developed—to the successive, "passing" time, the time generally wasted. On the contrary, essence incarnated in involuntary memory no longer grants us this original time. It causes us to regain time but in an altogether different fashion. What it causes us to regain is lost time itself. It suddenly supervenes, in a time already deployed, a developed time. Within this passing time, it regains a center of envelopment, which is however no longer anything but the image of original time. This is why the revelations of involuntary memory are extraordinarily brief and could not be extended without damage for us: "In the bewilderment of an uncertainty like the kind one experiences sometimes during an ineffable vision, at the moment of falling asleep" (III, 875). Reminiscence yields us the pure past, the past's very being in itself. No doubt this being transcends all the empirical dimensions of time. But in its very ambiguity, it is the principle starting from which these dimensions are deployed within lost time, as much as the principle in which we can regain that lost time itself, the center around which we can coil it anew in order to have an image of eternity. This pure past is the instance that is reduced to no "passing" present, but also the instance that makes every present pass, which presides over such passage: in this sense, it still implies the contradiction of survival and of nothingness. The ineffable vision is made of their mixture. Involuntary memory gives us eternity, but in such a manner that we do not have the strength to endure it for more than a moment nor the means to discover its nature. What it gives us is therefore rather the instantaneous image of eternity. And all the Selves of involuntary memory are inferior to the Self of art, from the viewpoint of essences themselves.

Lastly, the realization of essence in involuntary memory is not to be separated from determinations that remain external and contingent. That by virtue of the power of involuntary memory, something rises up in its essence or in its truth does not depend on circumstances. But that this "something" should be Combray, Balbec, or Venice; that it should be a certain essence (rather than some other) that is chosen, and which then finds the moment of its incarnation — this brings into play numerous circumstances and contingencies. On the one hand, it is obvious that the essence of Combray would not be realized in the recovered flavor of the madeleine, if there had not first been a real contiguity between the madeleine as it was tasted and Combray as it was present. On the other hand, the madeleine with its flavor and Combray with its qualities still have distinct substances that resist envelopment, resist mutual penetration.

We must therefore insist upon two points: an essence is incarnated in involuntary memory, but it finds there substances much less spiritualized, media less "dematerialized" than in art. And contrary to what happens in art, the choice of this essence then depends on data external to essence itself and refers in the last instance to experienced states, to mechanisms of associations that remain subjective and contingent. (Other contiguities would have induced or selected other essences.) In involuntary memory, physics emphasizes the resistance of substances; psychology emphasizes the irreducibility of subjective associations. This is why the signs of memory constantly ensnare us in an objectivist interpretation, but also and above all in the temptation of an altogether subjective interpretation. This is why, finally, reminiscences are inferior metaphors: instead of uniting two different objects whose choice and relation are entirely determined by an essence that is incarnated in a ductile or transparent medium, memory unites two objects that still depend on an opaque substance and whose relation depends upon an association. Thus essence itself is no longer master of its own incarnation, of its own choice, but is chosen according to data that remain external to it: essence thereby assumes that minimum of generality of which we spoke above.

This is to say that the sensuous signs of memory are signs of life, not of Art. Involuntary memory occupies a central place, not the extreme point. Such memory breaks with the attitude of conscious perception and of voluntary memory. It makes us sensitive to and gives us the interpretation of certain signs at privileged moments. The sensuous signs that correspond to involuntary memory are even superior to the worldly signs and to the signs of love. But they are inferior to other no less sensuous signs, signs of desire, of imagination or dreams (these latter already have more spiritual substances and refer to deeper associations that no longer depend on experienced contiguities). With all the more reason, the sensuous signs of involuntary memory are inferior to those of art; they have lost the perfect identity of sign and essence. They represent only the effort of life to prepare us for art and for the final revelation of art.

We must not regard art as a more profound means of exploring involuntary memory. We must regard involuntary memory as a stage, which is not even the most important stage, in the apprenticeship to art. It is certain that this memory sets us on the path of essences. Further, reminiscence already possesses essence, has been able to capture it. But it grants us essence in a slackened, secondary state and so obscurely that we are incapable of understanding the gift we are given and the joy we experience. To learn is to remember; but to remember is nothing more than to learn, to have a presentiment. If, impelled by the successive stages of the apprenticeship, we do not reach the final revelation of art, we shall remain incapable of understanding essence and even of understanding that it was already there within involuntary memory or within the joy of the sensuous sign (we should forever be reduced to "postponing" the examination of causes). All the stages must issue into art, we must reach the revelation of art; then we review the stages, we integrate them into the work of art itself, we recognize essence in its successive realizations, we give to each degree of realization the place and the meaning it occupies within the work. We discover then the role of involuntary memory and the reasons for this role, important but secondary in the incarnation of essences. The paradoxes of involuntary memory are explained by a higher instance, which overflows memory, inspires reminiscences, and communicates to them only a part of its secret.

CHAPTER 6

Series and Group

The incarnation of essences proceeds in the signs of love and even in the worldly signs. Difference and repetition remain then the two powers of essence, which itself remains irreducible to the object bearing the sign, but also to the subject experiencing it. Our loves are not explicated by those we love nor by our ephemeral states at the moment we are in love. But how are we to reconcile the idea of a presence of essence with the deceptive character of the signs of love and with the empty character of the signs of worldliness? It is because essence is led to assume an increasingly general form and an increasingly greater generality. At its limit, it tends to be identified with a "law" (it is apropos of love and worldliness that Proust likes to declare his penchant for generality, his passion for laws). Essences can therefore be incarnated in the signs of love, precisely as the general laws of the lie, and in the worldly signs, as the general laws of the void.

An original difference presides over our loves. Perhaps this is the image of the Mother — or that of the Father for a woman, for Mlle Vinteuil. More profoundly, it is a remote image beyond our experience, a Theme that transcends us, a kind of archetype. Image, idea, or essence rich enough to be diversified in the beings we love and even in a single loved being, but of such a nature too that it is repeated in our successive loves and in each of our loves taken in isolation. Albertine is the same and different, in relation to the hero's other loves, but also in relation to herself. There are so many Albertines that we should give a distinct name to each, and yet there is something like the same theme here, the same quality under various aspects. Reminiscences and discoveries mingle then in each love. Memory and imagination relieve and correct each other; each, taking a step, impels the other to take a supplementary step (I, 917–18). With all the more reason in our successive loves: each love contributes its difference, which was already included in the preceding love, and all the differences are contained in a primordial image that we unceasingly reproduce at different levels and repeat as the intelligible law of all our loves. "Thus my love for Albertine, and even as it differed from itself, was already inscribed within my love for Gilberte . . ." (III, 904).

In the signs of love, the two powers of essence are no longer united. The image or the theme contains the particular character of our loves. But we repeat this image only all the more, and all the better, in that it escapes us in fact and remains unconscious. Far from expressing the idea's immediate power, repetition testifies to a discrepancy here, an inadequation of consciousness and idea. Experience is no help to us because we deny that we repeat and still believe in something new, but also because we are unaware of the difference that makes our loves intelligible and refers them to a law that is in a sense their living source. The unconscious, in love, is the separation of the two aspects of essence: difference and repetition.

Love's repetition is a serial repetition. The hero's loves, for Gilberte, for Mme de Guermantes, for Albertine, form a series in which each term adds its minor difference. "At the very most, the woman we loved so much has added to this love a particular form, which will make us faithful to her even in our infidelity. We shall need, with the next woman, the same morning walks, or we shall need to take her home in the same way each night or to give her a hundred times too much money" (III, 908). But also, between two terms of the series, there appear certain relations of contrast that complicate the repetition. "Ah, how much my love for Albertine, whose fate I thought I could foresee according to the love I had had for Gilberte, had developed in utter contrast to the latter" (III, 447). And above all, when we pass from one loved term to the next, we must take into account a difference accumulated within the subject as well as a reason for progression in the series, "an index of variation that becomes more emphatic as we proceed into new regions, other latitudes of life" (I, 894). This is because the series, through minor differences and contrasting relations, ultimately converges upon its law, the lover himself constantly approaching a comprehension of the original theme. This comprehension he at last attains only when he has ceased to love, when he no longer has the desire or the time for love. It is in this sense that the series of loves is an apprenticeship: in its initial terms, love seems linked to its object, so that what is most important is avowal; later we learn love's subjectivity as well as the necessity of not avowing it in order to preserve our future loves. But as the series approaches its own law, and as our capacity to love approaches its own end, we realize the existence of the original theme or idea, which transcends our subjective states no less than the objects in which it is incarnated.

There is not only a series of successive loves; each love itself assumes a serial form. The minor differences and contrasting relations that we find from one love to another we already encounter in one and the same love: from one Albertine to another, because Albertine has many souls and many countenances. Precisely, these countenances and souls are not on the same plane; they are organized in series. (According to the law of contrast, "the minimum of variety... is of two. Recalling an energetic glance, a bold look, it is inevitably, the next time, by an almost languid profile, by a kind of dreamy gentleness — things we neglected in the preceding recollection — that we shall be startled and almost solely attracted" [III, 917–18].) Further, an index of subjective variation corresponds to each love; it measures its beginning, course, and termination. In all these senses, love for Albertine forms by itself a series in which are distinguished two different periods of jealousy. And at the end, the possibility of forgetting Albertine develops only insofar as the hero redescends the steps that marked the beginning of his love: "I realized now that before forgetting her altogether, before attaining that initial indifference, I would have to traverse in the opposite direction, like a traveler who returns by the same route to his starting point, all the feelings through which I had passed before reaching my great love" (III, 558). Thus three stages mark this forgetting, like an inverted series: the return to an undifferentiated perception, to a group of young girls analogous to the one from which Albertine was selected; the revelation of Albertine's tastes, which connects in a sense with the hero's first intuitions but at a moment when the truth can no longer interest him; finally the notion that Albertine is still alive, an idea that affords so little joy in contrast with the pain suffered when he knew she was dead and loved her still.

Not only does each love form a particular series, but at the other pole, the series of our loves transcends our experience, links up with other experiences, accedes to a transubjective reality. Swann's love for Odette already constitutes part of the series that continues with the hero's love for Gilberte, for Mme de Guermantes, for Albertine. Swann plays the part of an initiator, in a fate that he cannot realize on his own account: "After all, when I thought about it, the substance of my experience came to me from Swann, not only with regard to what concerned Swann himself and Gilberte. But it was Swann who since Combray had given me the desire to go to Balbec.... Without Swann I would not even have known the Guermantes..." (III, 915–16). Swann is here merely the occasion, but without this occasion the series would have been different. And in certain respects, Swann is much more. It is he who, from the start, possesses the law of the series or the secret of the progression and confides it to the hero in a "prophetic admonition": the beloved as Captive (I, 563).

We may locate the origin of this series in the hero's love for his mother, but here too we encounter Swann, who by coming to Combray to dine deprives the child of the maternal presence. And the anguish the hero suffers over his mother is already the anguish Odette caused Swann himself: "to him, that anguish of knowing our beloved is taking pleasure somewhere without us, where we cannot be—to him that anguish came through love, to which it is somehow predestined, by which it will be engrossed, monopolized; but when, as in my case, that anguish has entered into us before it has yet appeared in our lives, it hovers there, waiting for love, vague and unattached..." (I, 30). We will conclude from this that the image of the mother is perhaps not the most profound theme, nor the reason for the series of loves: it is true that our loves repeat our feelings for the mother, but the latter already repeat other loves, which we have not ourselves experienced. The mother appears rather as the transition from one experience to another, the way in which our experience begins but already links up with other experiences that were those of someone else. At its limit, the experience of love is that of all humanity, which is traversed by the current of a transcendent heredity.

Thus the personal series of our loves refers both to a vaster, transpersonal series and to more restricted series constituted by each love in particular. The series are thus implicated within each other, the indices of variation and the laws of progression enveloped within each other. When we ask how the signs of love are to be interpreted, we seek an instance by which the series may be explicated, the indices and the laws developed. Now, however great the role of memory and of imagination, these faculties intervene only on the level of each particular love, and less to interpret its signs than to surprise them and gather them up, in order to support a sensibility that apprehends them. The transition from one love to another finds its law in Forgetting, not in memory; in Sensibility, not in imagination. Actually, intelligence is the only faculty capable of interpreting the signs and explicating the series of loves. This is why Proust insists on the following point: there are realms in which the intelligence, supported by sensibility, is richer and more profound than memory and imagination (III, 900–902).

Not that the truths of love belong to those abstract truths that a thinker might discover by the effort of a method or of a free reflection. Intelligence must be forced, must undergo a constraint that leaves it no choice. This constraint is that of sensibility, that of the sign itself on the level of each love, because the signs of love are so many sorrows, because they always imply a lie on the part of the beloved, as a fundamental ambiguity by which our jealousy profits, on which it feeds. Then the suffering of our sensibility forces our intelligence to seek the meaning of the sign and the essence that is incarnated within it. "A sensitive man without imagination might even so write admirable novels. The suffering others cause him, his efforts to anticipate that suffering, the conflicts that suffering and the next cruel person create — all this, interpreted by the intelligence, might constitute the substance of a book... as fine as if it had been imagined, invented..." (III, 900–902).

In what does the intelligence's interpretation consist? It consists in discovering essence as the law of the series of loves. Which is to say, in the realm of love, essence is not to be separated from a strictly serial generality. Each suffering is particular, insofar as it is endured, insofar as it is produced by a specific being, at the heart of a specific love. But because these sufferings reproduce each other and implicate each other, the intelligence disengages from them something general, which is also a source of joy. The work of art "is a sign of happiness, because it teaches us that in any love the general borders on the particular, and to pass from the second to the first by a gymnastics that fortifies us against despair by helping us neglect its cause in order to intensify its essence" (III, 904). What we repeat is each time a particular suffering; but the repetition itself is always joyous, the phenomenon of repetition forms a general joy. Or rather, the phenomena are always unhappy and particular, but the idea extracted from them is general and joyous. For love's repetition is not to be separated from a law of progression by which we accede to a consciousness that transmutes our sufferings into joy. We realize that our sufferings do not depend on their object. They were "tricks" or "deceptions" we practiced on ourselves, or better still, snares and coquetries of the Idea, gaieties of Essence. There is something tragic about what is repeated but something comic in the repetition itself, and more profoundly, a joy of repetition understood or of the comprehension of its law. We extract from our particular despairs a general Idea; this is because the Idea was primary, was already there, as the law of the series is in its initial terms. The humor of the Idea is to manifest itself in despair, to appear itself as a kind of despair. Thus the end is already there in the beginning: "Ideas are the substitutes for sorrows. . . . Substitutes in the order of time only, moreover, for it seems that the initial element is the idea, and the sorrow merely the mode according to which certain ideas first enter into us" (III, 906).

Such is the operation of the intelligence: under a constraint of sensibility, it transmutes our suffering into joy at the same time that it transmutes the particular into the general. Only the intelligence can discover generality and find it a source of joy. It ultimately discovers what was present, but necessarily unconscious from the beginning: that the loved beings were not autonomously functioning causes but the terms of a series proceeding within us, the *tableaux vivants* of an internal theater, the reflections of an essence. "Each person who makes us suffer can be attached by us to a divinity of which that person is but a fragmentary reflection and the last degree, a divinity of whom the contemplation insofar as it is an idea immediately gives us joy instead of the pain we had suffered. The whole art of living is to make use of the persons who make us suffer as though of a stage permitting us to accede to that person's divine form, and thereby to people our lives, day by day, with divinities" (III, 899).

Essence is incarnated in the signs of love but necessarily in a serial, and hence a general, form. Essence is always difference. But, in love, the difference has passed into the unconscious: it becomes in a sense generic or specific and determines a repetition whose terms are no longer to be distinguished except by infinitesimal differences and subtle contrasts. In short, essence has assumed the generality of a Theme or an Idea, which serves as a law for the series of our loves. This is why the incarnation of essence, the choice of essence that is incarnated in the signs of love, depends on extrinsic conditions and subjective contingencies, even more than in the case of the sensuous signs. Swann is the great unconscious initiator, the point of departure for the series; but how can we help regretting the themes sacrificed, the essences eliminated, like the Leibnizian possibilities that do not pass into existence and would have given rise to other series in other circumstances and under other conditions? (III, 916). It is indeed the Idea that determines the series of our subjective states, but also it is the accidents of our subjective relations that determine the choice of the Idea. This is why the temptation of a subjectivist interpretation is even stronger in love than in the case of the sensuous signs: every love is linked to associations of ideas and impressions that are quite subjective, and the end of love is identified with the annihilation of a "portion" of associations, as in a stroke or when a weakened artery breaks (III, 592).

Nothing shows the externality of the choice better than the contingency that governs the identity of the beloved. Not only do our loves miscarry when we know perfectly well they might have succeeded had there been only the slightest difference in the circumstances (Mlle de Stermaria), but our loves that are realized, and the series that they form one after the next (by incarnating one essence rather than another), depend on occasions, on circumstances, on extrinsic factors.

One of the most striking cases is the following: the beloved belongs initially to a group, in which she is not yet individualized. Who will be the girl the hero loves in the homogeneous group? And by what accident is it that Albertine incarnates essence when another girl might have done so just as well? Or even another essence, incarnated in another girl, to whom the hero might have been sensitive, and who would have at least inflected the series of his loves? "Even now the sight of one of them gave me a pleasure that involved, to a degree I could not have expressed, seeing the others come along later on, and even if they did not appear on that day, talking about them and knowing that they would be told I had come to the beach" (I, 944). There is, in the group of young girls, a mixture, a conglomeration of essences, doubtless analogous, in relation to which the hero is almost equally accessible: "Each one of them had for me, as on the first day, something of the essence of the others" (II, 1113).

Albertine therefore enters the series of loves but only because she is selected from a group, with all the contingency that corresponds to this selection. The pleasures the hero experiences in the group are sensual pleasures. But these pleasures do not belong to love. In order to become a term in the series of loves, Albertine must be isolated from the group in which she first appears. She must be chosen; this choice is not made without uncertainty and contingency. Conversely, the hero's love for Albertine comes to an end only by a return to the group: either to the original group of young girls, as Andrée symbolizes it after Albertine's death ("at that moment it gave me pleasure to have a kind of carnal relationship with Andrée, because of the collective aspect that initially characterized my love for the girls of the little group, so long undifferentiated and reawakened now" [III, 596]); or to an analogous group, encountered in the street when Albertine is dead, which reproduces, but in the contrary direction, a formation of love, a choice of the beloved (III, 561–62). In a certain sense, group and series are in opposition; in another sense, they are inseparable and complementary.

Essence, as it is incarnated in the signs of love, is manifested successively in two aspects. First in the form of the general laws of deception. For it is necessary to lie — we are induced to lie — only to someone we love. If the lie obeys certain laws, it is because it implies a certain tension in the liar himself, a kind of system of physical relations between the truth and the denials or inventions by which the liar tries to conceal it: there are thus laws of contact, of attraction and repulsion, which form a veritable "physics" of deception. As a matter of fact, the truth is there, present in the beloved who lies; the beloved has a permanent knowledge of the truth, does not forget it, but quickly forgets an improvised lie. The hidden thing acts within the beloved in such a way that it extracts from its context a real but insignificant detail destined to guarantee the entirety of the lie. But it is precisely this little detail that betrays the beloved because its angles are not adapted to the rest, revealing another origin, a participation in another system. Or else the concealed thing acts at a distance, attracts the liar who unceasingly approaches it. He traces asymptotes, imagining he is making his secret insignificant by means of diminutive allusions, as when Charlus says, "I who have pursued beauty in all its forms." Or else we invent a host of likely details because we suppose that likelihood itself is an approximation of the truth, but then the excess of likelihood, like too many feet in a line of verse, betrays our lie and reveals the presence of what is false.

Not only does the concealed thing remain present in the liar, "for the most dangerous of all concealments is that of the deception itself in the mind of the guilty party" (II, 715). But because the concealed things unceasingly accumulate and grow larger like a black snowball, the liar is always betrayed; in effect, unconscious of this progression, he maintains the same discrepancy between what he avows and what he denies. Since what he denies increases, he increasingly avows as well. In the liar himself, the perfect lie would suppose a prodigious memory oriented toward the future, capable of leaving traces in the future, as much as the truth would. And above all, the lie would require being "total." These conditions are not of this world; thus lies and deceptions belong to signs. They are, precisely, the signs of those truths that they claim to conceal: "Illegible and divine vestiges" (I, 279). Illegible, but not inexplicable or without interpretation.

The beloved woman conceals a secret, even if it is known to everyone else. The lover himself conceals the beloved: a powerful jailer. We must be harsh, cruel, and deceptive with those we love. Indeed, the lover lies no less than the beloved; he sequesters her, and also is careful not to avow his love to her, in order to remain a better guardian, a better jailer. Now, the essential thing for the woman is to conceal the origin of the worlds she implicates in herself, the point of departure of her gestures, her habits and tastes that she temporarily devotes to us. The beloved women are oriented toward a secret of Gomorrah as toward an original sin: "Albertine's hideousness" (III, 610). But the lovers themselves have a corresponding secret, an analogous hideousness. Conscious or not, it is the secret of Sodom. So the truth of love is dualistic, and the series of loves, only apparently simple, is divided into two others, more profound, represented by Mlle Vinteuil and by Charlus. The hero of the Search therefore has two overwhelming revelations when, in analogous circumstances, he surprises Mlle Vinteuil, then Charlus (II, 608). What do these two homosexual series signify?

Proust tries to tell us in the passage of *Sodome et Gomorrhe*, in which a vegetal metaphor constantly recurs. The truth of love is first of all the isolation of the sexes. We live under Samson's prophecy: "The two sexes shall die, each in a place apart" (II, 616). But matters are complicated because the separated, partitioned sexes coexist in the same individual: "initial Hermaphroditism," as in a plant or a snail, which cannot be fertilized "except by other hermaphrodites" (II, 629). Then it happens that the intermediary, instead of effecting the communication of male and female, doubles each sex with itself: symbol of a self-fertilization all the more moving in that it is homosexual, sterile, indirect. And more than an episode, this is the essence of love. The original Hermaphrodite continuously produces the two divergent homosexual series. It separates the sexes, instead of uniting them — to the point where men and women meet only in appearance. It is of all lovers, and all women loved, that we must affirm what becomes obvious only in certain special cases: the lovers "play for the woman who loves women the role of another woman, and the woman offers them at the same time an approximation of what they find in a man" (II, 622).

Essence, in love, is incarnated first in the laws of deception, but second in the secrets of homosexuality: deception would not have the generality that renders it essential and significant if it did not refer to homosexuality as the truth that it conceals. All lies are organized around homosexuality, revolving around it as around their center. Homosexuality is the truth of love. This is why the series of loves is really double: it is organized in two series that find their source not only in the images of mother and father, but in a more profound phylogenetic continuity. Initial Hermaphroditism is the continuous law of the divergent series; from one series to the other, we see love constantly engendering *signs* that are those of Sodom and Gomorrah.

Generality signifies two things: either the law of a series (or of several series) whose terms differ, or else the character of a group whose elements resemble each other. And doubtless the groups intervene in love. The lover extracts the beloved being from a previous group, and interprets signs that are initially collective. Better still, the women of Gomorrah or the men of Sodom emit "astral signs," according to which they recognize each other, and form accursed associations that reproduce the two Biblical cities (II, 852). The fact remains that the group is not the essential thing in love; it only affords occasions. The true generality of love is serial; our loves are experienced profoundly only according to the series in which they are organized. The same is not true in the case of worldliness. Essences are still incarnated in the worldly signs, but at a last level of contingency and generality. They are immediately incarnated in societies, their generality is no more than a group generality: *the last degree of essence.*

Doubtless the "world" expresses social, historical, and political forces. But the worldly signs are emitted in a void. Thereby, they traverse astronomic distances, so that observation of worldliness bears no resemblance to study by microscope, but rather to study by telescope. And Proust often says as much: at a certain level of essences, what interests him is no longer individuality or detail, but laws, great distances, and major generalities. The telescope, not the microscope (III, 1041). This is already true of love, and with all the more reason, of "the world." The void is precisely a generality-bearing milieu, a physical milieu accommodating for the manifestation of a law. An empty head offers better statistical laws than a denser matter: "The stupidest beings, by their gestures, their remarks, their involuntarily expressed sentiments, manifest laws that they do not perceive, but which the artist surprises in them" (III, 901). Doubtless it happens that a singular genius, a master-soul, presides over the course of the stars: thus Charlus. But just as the astronomers have ceased believing in master-souls, the world itself ceases to believe in Charlus. The laws that preside over the changes of the world are mechanical laws, in which Forgetting prevails. (In a series of famous pages, Proust analyzes the power of social forgetting in terms of the evolution of the Parisian salons from the Dreyfus Affair to the First World War. Few texts constitute a better commentary on Lenin's remark as to a society's capacity to replace "the corrupt old prejudices" by new prejudices even more infamous or more stupid.)

Vacuity, stupidity, forgetfulness: such is the trinity of the worldly group. But worldliness thereby gains a speed, a mobility in the emission of signs, a perfection in formalism, a generality in meaning: all things that make it a necessary milieu for apprenticeship. As essence is incarnated ever more loosely, the signs assume a comic power. They provoke in us a kind of increasingly external nervous exaltation; they excite the intelligence, in order to be interpreted. For nothing gives more food for thought than what goes on in the head of a fool. Those who are like parrots, in a group, are also "prophetic birds": their chatter indicates the presence of a law (II, 236). And if the groups still afford a rich substance for interpretation, it is because they possess concealed affinities, a strictly unconscious content. The true families, the true milieus, the true groups are "intellectual." Which is to say, one always belongs to the society that emits the ideas and the values one believes in. In invoking the immediate influence of milieus that are simply physical and real, Taine or Sainte-Beuve errs, and this error is not the least. Actually, the interpreter must reconstruct the groups by discovering the *mental* families to which they are attached. It happens that duchesses, or M. de Guermantes himself, speak like *petit-bourgeois*: this is because the law of the world, and more generally the law of language, is "that one always expresses oneself like the people of one's mental class and not of one's caste of origin" (III, 900).

CHAPTER 7

Pluralism in the System of Signs

The search for lost time is presented as a system of signs. But this system is pluralistic. Not only because the classification of signs involves many criteria, but because we must combine two distinct viewpoints in the establishment of these criteria. On the one hand, we must consider the signs from the viewpoint of an apprenticeship in process. What is the power and effectiveness of each type of sign? In other words, to what degree does it help to prepare us for the final revelation? What does it make us understand, in and of itself and at the moment, according to a law of progression that varies according to types and refers to other types according to rules that are themselves variable? On the other hand, we must consider the signs from the viewpoint of the final revelation. This revelation is identified with Art, the highest kind of signs. But, in the work of art, all the other signs are included; they find a place according to the effectiveness they had in the course of the apprenticeship—find, even, an ultimate explanation of the characteristics they then afforded, which we experienced without being able to comprehend them fully.

Taking these viewpoints into account, the system involves seven criteria. The first five can be briefly reviewed; the last two have consequences that must be developed.

1. The matter in which the sign is embodied. These substances are more or less resistant and opaque, more or less dematerialized, more or less spiritualized. The worldly signs, though they function in a void, are only the more material for that. The signs of love are inseparable from the weight of a face, from the texture of a skin, from the width and color of a cheek—things that are spiritualized only when the beloved sleeps. The sensuous signs are still material qualities, above all odors and tastes. It is only in art that the sign becomes immaterial at the same time that its meaning becomes spiritual.

2. *The way in which something is emitted and apprehended as a sign, but also the consequent dangers of an interpretation that may be objectivist or subjectivist.* Each type of sign refers us to the object that emits it and also to the subject who apprehends and interprets it. We believe at first that we must see and hear; or else, in love, that we must avow our love (pay homage to the object); or else that we must observe and describe the sensuous phenomenon; that we must work, must think in order to grasp significations and objective values. Disappointed, we fall back into the play of subjective associations. But for each kind of sign, these two moments of the apprenticeship have a rhythm and specific relations.

3. *The effect of the sign upon us, the kind of emotion it produces.* Nervous exaltation is produced by the worldly signs; suffering and anguish by the signs of love; extraordinary joy by the sensuous signs (but in which anguish still appears as the subsisting contradiction of being and nothingness); pure joy by the signs of art.

4. *The nature of meaning, and the sign's relation to its meaning.* The worldly signs are empty; they take the place of action and thought; they try to stand for their meaning. The signs of love are deceptive; their meaning inheres in

the contradiction of what they reveal and try to conceal. The sensuous signs are truthful, but in them subsists the opposition of survival and nothingness, and their meaning is still material; it resides elsewhere. However, to the degree that we achieve art, the relation of sign and meaning becomes closer. Art is the splendid final unity of an immaterial sign and a spiritual meaning.

5. *The principal faculty that explicates or interprets the sign, which develops its meaning.* This faculty is intelligence, in the case of the worldly signs; intelligence, too, but in another fashion, in the case of the signs of love (the effort of intelligence is no longer supported by an exaltation that must be calmed, but by the sufferings of sensibility that must be transmuted into joy). In the case of the sensuous signs, it is involuntary memory and imagination as the latter is generated by desire. In the case of the signs of art, pure thought as the faculty of essences becomes the interpreter.

6. *The temporal structures or lines of time implicated in the sign, and the corresponding type of truth.* It always takes time to interpret a sign; all time is the time of an interpretation, that is, of a development. In the case of the worldly signs, we waste our time, for these signs are empty, and at the end of their development we find they are intact or identical. Like the monster, like the spiral, they are reborn from their metamorphoses. Nonetheless such wasted time has a truth: a kind of maturation of the interpreter who does not find *himself* to be identical. In the case of the signs of love, we are mainly within time lost: time that alters persons and things, that makes them pass. Here too

there is a truth — or truths. But the truth of lost time is not only approximate and equivocal; we grasp it only when it has ceased to interest us, only when the interpreter's Self that was in love has already disappeared. So it is with Gilberte, so it is with Albertine: in love, the truth always comes too late. Love's time is a lost time because the sign develops only to the degree that the self corresponding to its meaning disappears. The sensuous signs offer us a new structure of time: time rediscovered at the heart of lost time itself, an image of eternity. This is because the sensuous signs (unlike the signs of love) have the power either to awaken by desire and imagination or to reawaken by involuntary memory the Self that corresponds to their meaning. Lastly, the signs of art define time regained: an absolute primordial time, a veritable eternity that unites sign and meaning.

Time wasted, time lost, time rediscovered, and time regained are the four lines of time. But we must note that if each type of sign has its particular line, it participates in the other lines as well, encroaches on them as it develops. *It is therefore on the lines of time that the signs intersect and multiply their combinations.* Time wasted is extended in all the other signs except the signs of art. Conversely, time lost is already present in the worldly signs; it transforms and compromises them in their formal identity. It is also there, subjacent, in the sensuous signs, introducing a sense of nothingness even in the joys of sensibility. Time rediscovered, in its turn, is not alien to time lost; we encounter it at the very heart of time lost. Lastly, the time regained by art encompasses and comprehends all the others, for it is only within time regained that each line of time finds its truth, its place, and its result from the viewpoint of truth.

From a certain viewpoint, each line of time is valid in itself ("all these different planes on which Time, now that I had just regained possession of it during this party, arranged my life..." [III, 1031]). These temporal structures are therefore like "different and parallel series" (II, 757). But this parallelism or autonomy of the various series does not exclude, from another viewpoint, a kind of hierarchy. From one line to another, the relation of sign and meaning becomes more intimate, more necessary, and more profound. In every instance, on the higher line, we recover what remained lost on the others. It is as if the lines of time broke off and fit into each other. Thus it is Time itself that is serial; each aspect of time is now itself a term of the absolute temporal series and refers to a Self that possesses an increasingly vast and increasingly individualized field of exploration. The primordial time of art imbricates all the different kinds of time; the absolute Self of art encompasses all the different kinds of Self.

7. *Essence.* From the worldly signs to the sensuous signs, the relation between the sign and its meaning is increasingly intimate. Thus there appears what the philosophers would call an "ascending dialectic." But it is only at the profoundest level, on the level of art, that Essence is revealed: as the reason for this relation and for its variations. Then, starting from this final revelation, we can redescend the steps. Not that we would go back into life, into love, into worldliness, but we redescend the series of time by assigning to each temporal line, and to each

species of signs, the truth appropriate to them. When we have reached the revelation of art, we learn that essence was already there, in the lowest steps and stages. It is essence that, in each case, determined the relation between sign and meaning. This relation was all the closer when essence was incarnated with more necessity and individuality; all the looser, on the contrary, when essence assumed a greater generality and was incarnated in more contingent data. Thus, in art, essence individualizes the subject in which it is incorporated, and absolutely determines the objects that express it. But in the sensuous signs, essence begins to assume a minimum of generality; its incarnation depends on contingent data and external determinations. Even more so in the case of the signs of love and the worldly signs: the generality of essence is then a generality of series or a generality of group; its choice refers increasingly to extrinsic objective determinations, to subjective mechanisms of association. This is why we could not understand, at the moment, that Essences already animated the worldly signs, signs of love, and sensuous signs. But once the signs of art have given us the revelation of essence in their own regard, we recognize its effect in the other realms. We can recognize the marks of its attenuated, loosened splendor. Then we are in a position to render essence its due, and to recover all the truths of time, and all the kinds of signs, in order to make them integral parts of the work of art itself.

Implication and explication, envelopment and development: such are the categories of the Search. First of all, meaning is implicated in the sign; it is like one thing wrapped within another. The captive, the captive soul signify that there is always an involution, an involvement of the diverse. The signs emanate from objects that are like boxes or containers. The objects hold a captive soul, the soul of something else that tries to open the lid (I, 179). Proust favors "the Celtic belief that the souls of those we have lost are imprisoned in some inferior being, in an animal, a plant, an inanimate thing; lost indeed to us until the day, which for many never comes, when we happen to approach the tree, to come into possession of the object that is their prison" (I, 44). But the metaphors of implication correspond further to the images of explication. For the sign develops, uncoils at the same time that it is interpreted. The jealous lover develops the possible worlds enclosed within the beloved. The sensitive man liberates the souls implicated in things, somewhat as we see the pieces of Japanese paper flower in the water, expanding or extending, forming blossoms, houses, and characters (I, 47). Meaning itself is identified with this development of the sign as the sign was identified with the involution of meaning. So that Essence is finally the third term that dominates the other two, that presides over their movement: essence complicates the sign and the meaning; it holds them *in complication*; it puts the one in the other. It measures in each case their relation, their degree of distance or proximity, the degree of their unity. Doubtless the sign itself is not reduced to the object, but the object still sheaths half of it. Doubtless the meaning by itself is not reduced to the subject, but it half depends on the subject, on subjective circumstances and associations. Beyond

the sign and the meaning, there is Essence, like the sufficient reason for the other two terms and for their relation.

What is essential in the Search is not memory and
time, but the sign and truth. What is essential is not to remember, but to learn. For memory is valid only as a faculty capable of interpreting certain signs; time is valid only
as the substance or type of this or that truth. And memory, whether voluntary or involuntary, intervenes only at
specific moments of the apprenticeship, in order to con-
centrate its effect or to open a new path. The notions of
the Search are: sign, meaning, and essence; the continuity of apprenticeship and the abruptness of revelation.
That Charlus is homosexual is an astonishment. But the
interpreter's continuous and gradual maturation was required for the qualitative leap into a new knowledge, a
new realm of signs. The leitmotifs of the Search are: *I did
not yet know, I was to understand later*; and also, *I was no
longer interested once I ceased to learn.* The characters of the
Search have importance only insofar as they emit signs to
be deciphered, according to a more or less profound rhythm
of time. The grandmother, Françoise, Mme de Guermantes, Charlus, Albertine — each is valid only by what
he or she teaches us. "The joy with which I ventured upon
my first apprenticeship when Françoise...." "From Albertine I had nothing more to learn...."

There is a Proustian vision of the world. It is defined
initially by what it excludes: crude matter, mental delib-
eration, physics, philosophy. Philosophy supposes direct
declaration and explicit signification, proceeding from a
mind seeking the truth. Physics supposes an objective and

unambiguous matter subject to the conditions of reality. We are wrong to believe in facts; there are only signs. We are wrong to believe in truth; there are only interpretations. The sign is an ever-equivocal, implicit, and implicated meaning. "I had followed in my existence a progress that was the converse of that of the races of the world, which employed phonetic writing only after having considered the characters as a series of symbols" (III, 88). What unites the scent of a flower and the spectacle of a salon, the taste of a madeleine and the emotion of love is the sign and the corresponding apprenticeship. The scent of a flower, when it constitutes a sign, transcends at once the laws of matter and the categories of mind. We are not physicists or metaphysicians; we must be Egyptologists. For there are no mechanical laws between things or voluntary communications between minds. Everything is implicated, everything is complicated, everything is sign, meaning, essence. Everything exists in those obscure zones that we penetrate as into crypts, in order to decipher hieroglyphs and secret languages. The Egyptologist, in all things, is the man who undergoes an initiation—the apprentice.

Neither things nor minds exist, there are only bodies: astral bodies, vegetal bodies. The biologists would be right if they knew that bodies in themselves are already a language. The linguists would be right if they knew that language is always the language of bodies. Every symptom is a word, but first of all every word is a symptom. "Words themselves instructed me only if they were interpreted in the fashion of a rush of blood to the face of a person who is disturbed, or again in the fashion of a sudden silence" (III, 88). It will come as no surprise that the hysteric makes his body speak. He rediscovers a primary language, the true language of symbols and hieroglyphs. His body is an Egypt. Mme Verdurin's gestures, her fear that her jaw will come unhinged, her artistic posturings that resemble those of sleep, her medicated nose, these constitute an alphabet for the initiated.

The Image of Thought

If time has great importance in the Search, it is because every truth is a truth of time. But the Search is first of all a search for truth. Thereby is manifested the "philosophical" bearing of Proust's work: it vies with philosophy. Proust sets up an image of thought in opposition to that of philosophy. He attacks what is most essential in a classical philosophy of the rationalist type: the presuppositions of this philosophy. The philosopher readily presupposes that the mind as mind, the thinker as thinker, wants the truth, loves or desires the truth, naturally seeks the truth. He assumes in advance the goodwill of thinking; all his investigation is based on a "premeditated decision." From this comes the method of philosophy: from a certain viewpoint, the search for truth would be the most natural and the easiest; the decision to undertake it and the possession of a method capable of overcoming the external influences that distract the mind from its vocation and cause it to take the false for the true would suffice. It would be a matter of discovering and organizing ideas according to an order of thought, as so many explicit significations or formulated truths, which would then fulfill the search and assure agreement between minds.

In the "philosopher" there is the "friend." It is important that Proust offers the same critique of philosophy as of friendship. Friends are, in relation to one another, like minds of goodwill who are in agreement as to the signification of things and words; they communicate under the effect of a mutual goodwill. Philosophy is like the expression of a Universal Mind that is in agreement with itself in order to determine explicit and communicable significations. Proust's critique touches the essential point: truths remain arbitrary and abstract so long as they are based on the goodwill of thinking. Only the conventional is explicit. This is because philosophy, like friendship, is ignorant of the dark regions in which are elaborated the effective forces that act on thought, the determinations that *force* us to think; a friend is not enough for us to approach the truth. Minds communicate to each other only the conventional; the mind engenders only the possible. The truths of philosophy are lacking in necessity and the mark of necessity. As a matter of fact, the truth is not revealed, it is betrayed; it is not communicated, it is interpreted; it is not willed, it is involuntary.

The great theme of *Time regained* is that the search for truth is the characteristic adventure of the involuntary. Thought is nothing without something that forces and does violence to it. More important than thought is "what leads to thought"; more important than the philosopher is the poet. Victor Hugo writes philosophy in his first poems because he "still thinks, instead of being content, like nature, to lead to thought" (II, 549). But the poet learns that what is essential is outside of thought, in what forces us to think. The *leitmotif* of *Time regained* is the word *force*: impressions that force us to look, encounters that force us to interpret, expressions that force us to think. "The truths that intelligence grasps directly in the open light of day have something less profound, less *nec-*

essary about them than those that life has communicated to us *in spite of ourselves* in an impression, a material impression because it has reached us through our senses, but whose spirit we can extract.... I would have to try to interpret the sensations as the *signs* of so many laws and ideas, by attempting to think, that is, to bring out of the darkness what I had felt, and convert it into a spiritual equivalent.... Whether this was a matter of reminiscences of the kind that included the noise of the fork or the taste of the madeleine, or of those truths written with the help of figures whose meaning I was trying to discover in my mind, where, like steeples or weeds, they composed a complicated and elaborate *herbal*, their first character was that *I was not free* to choose them, that they were given to me as they were. And I felt that this must be the mark of their authenticity. *I had not gone looking* for the two cobblestones of the courtyard where I had stumbled. But precisely the *fortuitous, inevitable* way in which the sensation had been *encountered* governed the truth of the past that it resuscitated, of the images that it released, because we feel its effort to rise toward the light, because we feel the joy of reality regained.... In order to read the inner book of these unknown *signs* (signs in relief, it seemed, which my attention would seek out, would bump into, would pass by, like a diver exploring the depths), no one could help me by any rules, such reading consisting in an act of creation in which nothing can take our place or even collaborate with us.... The ideas formed by pure intelligence have only a logical truth, a possible truth, their choice is arbitrary. The book whose characters are figured, *not traced by us*, is our only book. Not that the ideas we form cannot be logically exact, but we do not know whether they are true. Only the impression, however paltry their substance seems, however unlikely their traces, is a criterion of truths and on this account alone merits being apprehended by the mind, for only the impression is capable, if the mind can disengage this truth from it, of leading the mind to a greater perfection and of giving it a pure joy" (III, 878–80).

What forces us to think is the sign. The sign is the object of an encounter, but it is precisely the contingency of the encounter that guarantees the necessity of what it leads us to think. The act of thinking does not proceed from a simple natural possibility; on the contrary, it is the only true creation. Creation is the genesis of the act of thinking within thought itself. This genesis implicates something that does violence to thought, which wrests it from its natural stupor and its merely abstract possibilities. To think is always to interpret—to explicate, to develop, to decipher, to translate a sign. Translating, deciphering, developing are the form of pure creation. There is no more an explicit signification than a clear idea. There are only meanings implicated in signs; and if thought has the power to explicate the sign, to develop it in an Idea, this is because the Idea is already there in the sign, in the enveloped and involuted state, in the obscure state of what forces us to think. We seek the truth only within time, constrained and forced. The truth seeker is the jealous man who catches a lying sign on the beloved's face. He is the sensitive man, in that he encounters the violence of an impression. He is the reader, the auditor, in that the work of art emits signs that will perhaps force him to create, like the call of genius to other geniuses. The communications of garrulous friendship are nothing compared to a lover's silent interpretations. Philosophy, with all its method and its goodwill, is nothing compared to the secret pressures of the work of art. Creation, like the genesis of the act of thinking, always starts from signs. The work of art is born from signs as much as it generates them; the creator is like the jealous man, interpreter of the god, who scrutinizes the signs in which the truth *betrays itself.*

The adventure of the involuntary recurs on the level of each faculty. In two different ways, the worldly signs and the signs of love are interpreted by the intelligence. But this is no longer that abstract and voluntary intelligence, which claims to find logical truths by itself, to have its own order, and to anticipate pressures from the outside world. This is an involuntary intelligence, the intelligence that undergoes the pressure of signs and comes to life only in order to interpret them, in order thus to exorcise the void in which it chokes, the suffering that submerges it. In science and in philosophy, the intelligence always "comes before," but characteristic of signs is their appeal to the intelligence insofar as it comes after, insofar as it must come after (III, 880). The same is true of memory; the sensuous signs force us to seek the truth, but thereby mobilize an involuntary memory (or an involuntary imagination born of desire). Finally the signs of art force us to think; they mobilize pure thought as a faculty of essences. They release within thought what depends least on its goodwill: the act of thinking itself. The signs mobilize, constrain a faculty: intelligence, memory, or imagination. This faculty, in its turn, mobilizes thought, forces it to conceive essences. Under the signs of art, we learn what pure thought is as a faculty of essences and how the intelligence, the memory, or the imagination diversify it in relation to the other kinds of signs.

Voluntary and involuntary do not designate different faculties, but rather a different exercise of the same faculties. Perception, memory, imagination, intelligence, and thought itself have only a contingent exercise as long as they are exercised voluntarily; so what we perceive, we could just as well remember, imagine, or conceive, and conversely. Neither perception, nor voluntary memory, nor voluntary thought gives us profound truth, but only possible truths. Here, nothing forces us to interpret something, to decipher the nature of a sign, or to dive deep like "the diver who explores the depths." All the faculties are harmoniously exercised, but one in place of the other, in the arbitrary and in the abstract. On the contrary, each time that a faculty assumes its involuntary form, it discovers and attains its own limit, it rises to a transcendent exercise, it understands its own necessity as well as its irreplaceable power. It ceases to be interchangeable. Instead of an indifferent perception, a sensibility that apprehends and receives signs, the sign is the limit of this sensibility, its vocation, its extreme exercise. Instead of a voluntary intelligence, a voluntary memory, a voluntary imagination, all these faculties appear in their involuntary and transcendent form; then each one discovers that it alone can interpret, each explicates a type of sign that does it particular violence. Involuntary exercise is the transcendent limit or the vocation of each faculty. Instead of voluntary thought, it is all that forces us to think, all that is forced to think, all of involuntary thought that can conceive only essences. Only the sensibility grasps the sign as such; only intelligence, memory, or imagination explicates the meaning, each according to a certain kind of sign; only pure thought discovers essence, is forced to conceive essence as the sufficient reason of the sign and its meaning.

It may be that Proust's critique of philosophy is eminently philosophical. What philosopher would not hope to set up an image of thought that no longer depends on the goodwill of the thinker and on a premeditated decision? Each time we propose a concrete and dangerous thought, we know that it does not depend on an explicit decision or method but on an encountered, refracted violence that leads us in spite of ourselves to Essences. For the essences dwell in dark regions, not in the temperate zones of the clear and the distinct. They are involved in what forces us to think; they do not answer to our voluntary effort; they let themselves be conceived only if we are forced to do so.

Proust is a Platonist, but not in the vague sense, not because he invokes essences or Ideas apropos of Vinteuil's little phrase. Plato offers us an image of thought under the sign of encounters and violences. In a passage of the *Republic*, Plato distinguishes two kinds of things in the world: those that leave the mind inactive or give it only the pretext of an appearance of activity, and those that lead it to think, which force us to think (VII, 523b–25b). The first are the objects of recognition; all the faculties are exercised upon these objects, but in a contingent exercise, which makes us say "that is a finger," that is an apple, that is a house, and so on. Conversely, other things force us to think: no longer *recognizable* objects, but things that do violence, *encountered* signs. These are "simultaneously contrary perceptions," Plato states. (Proust will say: sensations common to two places, to two moments.) The sensuous sign does us violence: it mobilizes the memory, it sets the soul in motion; but the soul in its turn excites thought, transmits to it the constraint of the sensibility, forces it to conceive essence, as the only thing that must be conceived. Thus the faculties enter into a transcendent exercise, in which each confronts and joins its own limit: the sensibility that apprehends the sign; the soul, the memory, that interprets it; the mind that is forced to conceive essence. Socrates can rightly say: I am Love more than the friend, I am the lover; I am art more than philosophy; I am constraint and violence, rather than goodwill. The *Symposium*, the *Phaedrus*, and the *Phaedo* are the three great studies of signs.

But the Socratic demon, irony, consists in anticipating the encounters. In Socrates, the intelligence still comes before the encounters; it provokes them, it instigates and organizes them. Proust's humor is of another nature: Jewish humor as opposed to Greek irony. One must be endowed for the signs, ready to encounter them, one must open oneself to their violence. The intelligence always comes after; it is good when it comes after; it is good only when it comes after. As we have seen, this distinction between Proust and Platonism involved many more differences. *There is no Logos; there are only hieroglyphs.* To think is therefore to interpret, is therefore to translate. The essences are at once the thing to be translated and the translation itself, the sign and the meaning. They are involved in the sign in order to force us to think; they develop in the meaning in order to be necessarily conceived. The hieroglyph is everywhere; its double symbol is the accident of the encounter and the necessity of thought: "fortuitous and inevitable."

Part II. The Literary Machine

CHAPTER 8

Antilogos

Proust has his own way of experiencing the opposition of Athens and Jerusalem. He eliminates many things or many people in the course of the Search, and these form an apparently incongruous group: observers, friends, philosophers, talkers, homosexuals *à la grecque*, intellectuals. But all of them participate in the *logos*, and are with varying qualifications the characters of a single universal dialectic: the dialectic as Conversation among Friends, in which all faculties are exercised voluntarily and collaborate under the leadership of the Intelligence, in order to unite the observation of Things, the discovery of Laws, the formation of Words, the analysis of Ideas, and to weave that perpetual web linking Part to Whole and Whole to Part. To observe each thing as a whole, then to discover its law as part of a whole, which is itself present by its Ideal in each of its parts — is this not the universal logos, that totalizing impulse we variously recognize in the conversation of friends, in the analytic and rational truth of philosophers, in the methods of scientists and scholars, in the concerted work of art of *littérateurs*, in the conventional symbolism of words themselves?[1]

There is one aspect, however concealed it may be, of the logos, by means of which the Intelligence always *comes before*, by which the whole is already present, the law already known before what it applies to: this is the dialectical trick by which we discover only what we have already given ourselves, by which we derive from things only what we have already put there. (Thus we will recognize the vestiges of a Logos in Sainte-Beuve and his detestable method when he interrogates an author's friends in order to evaluate his writing as the effect of a family, a period, a milieu, even if Sainte-Beuve also considers the work in its turn as a whole that reacts on its milieu. It is a method that leads him to treat Baudelaire and Stendhal somewhat in the way Socrates treats Alcibiades: as nice boys well worth knowing. Goncourt too employs crumbs of the Logos, when he observes the Verdurin dinner party and the guests gathered "for entirely superior conversations mingled with parlor games.")[2]

The Search is constructed on a series of oppositions: Proust counters observation with sensibility, philosophy with thought, reflection with translation. He counters the logical or conjoined use of all our faculties — preceded by the intelligence that brings them all together in the fiction of a "total soul" — by a nonlogical and disjunct use, which shows that we never command all our faculties at once and that intelligence always *comes after*.[3] Further, Proust counters friendship with love, conversation with silent interpretation, Greek homosexuality with the Biblical and accursed variety, words with names, explicit significations with implicit signs and involuted meanings. "I had followed a course contrary to that of humanity that employs phonetic writing only after having regarded the letters as a series of symbols; I who had so long sought the real life and thought of others only in the direct utterance they voluntarily afforded me — I had now been brought, and by just those others, to attach importance only to the testimony, on the contrary, which is not a rational and analytic expression of the truth; words themselves taught me something only if they were interpreted in the fashion of a rush of blood to the face of a person who is disturbed, or again in the fashion of a sudden silence" (III, 88). Not that Proust substitutes for the logic of Truth a simple psychophysiology of motifs. It is indeed the being of truth that forces us to seek it in what is implicated or complicated and not in the clear images and manifest ideas of the intelligence.

Let us consider three secondary characters of the Search who, each by specific aspects, relate to the Logos: Saint-Loup, an intellectual who is passionate about friendship; Norpois, obsessed by the conventional significations of diplomacy; Cottard, who has concealed his timidity with the cold mask of authoritarian scientific discourse. Now each in his way reveals the bankruptcy of the Logos and has value only because of his familiarity with mute, fragmentary, and subjacent signs that integrate him into some part of the Search. Cottard, an illiterate fool, finds his genius in diagnosis, the interpretation of ambiguous syndromes (I, 433, 497–99). Norpois knows perfectly well that the conventions of diplomacy, like those of worldliness, mobilize and restore pure signs under the explicit significations employed.[4] Saint-Loup explains that the art of war depends less on science and reasoning than on the penetration of signs that are always partial, ambiguous signs enveloped by heterogeneous factors, or even false signs intended to deceive the adversary (II, 114). There is no Logos of war, of politics, or of surgery, but only ciphers coiled within substances and fragments that are not totalizable and make the strategist, the diplomat, and the physician themselves so many odd fragments of a divine interpreter closer to the parlor sibyl than to the learned dialectician. Everywhere Proust contrasts the world of signs and symptoms with the world of attributes, the world of pathos with the world of logos, the world of hieroglyphs and ideograms with the world of analytic expression, phonetic writing, and rational thought. What is constantly impugned are the great themes inherited from the Greeks: *philos, sophia, dialogue, logos, phoné.* And it is only the rats in our nightmares that "pronounce Ciceronian orations." The world of signs is contrasted with the Logos from five viewpoints: the configuration of the parts as they are outlined in the world, the nature of the law they reveal, the use of the faculties they solicit, the type of unity they create, and the structure of the language that translates and interprets them. It is from all these viewpoints — parts, law, use, unity, style — that we must set the sign in opposition to the logos and from which we must contrast pathos and logos.

As we have seen, however, there is a certain Platonism in Proust: the entire Search is an experimentation with reminiscences and essences. And the disjunct use of the faculties in their involuntary exercise has, as we know, its model in Plato's education of a sensibility open to the violence of signs, a remembering soul that interprets them and discovers their meaning, an intelligence that discerns essence. But an obvious difference appears: Plato's reminiscence has its point of departure in sensuous qualities or relations apprehended in process, in variation, in opposition, in "mutual fusion." But this qualitative transition represents a state of things, a state of the world that imitates the Idea as best it can, according to its powers. And the Idea as the goal of reminiscence is the stable Essence, the thing in itself separating opposites, introducing the perfect mean into the whole. This is why the Idea is always "before," always presupposed, even when it is discovered only afterwards. The point of departure is valid only in its capacity to imitate, already, the goal, so that the disjunct use of the faculties is merely a "prelude" to the dialectic that unites them in a single Logos, as the construction of arcs prepares us to draw an entire circle. As Proust says, summarizing his whole critique of the dialectic, the Intelligence always comes "before."

This is not at all true in the Search: qualitative transition, mutual fusion, and "unstable opposition" are inscribed within a *state of soul*, no longer within a state of things or a state of the world. A slanting ray of the setting sun, an odor, a flavor, a draft, an ephemeral qualitative complex owes its value only to the "subjective aspect" that it penetrates. This is in fact why the reminiscence intervenes: because the quality is inseparable from a chain of subjective associations, which we are not free to experiment with the first time we experience it. Of course, the subjective aspect is never the last word of the Search; Swann's weakness is that he proceeds no further than simple associations, captive of his moods, his "states of soul," associating Vinteuil's little phrase with the love he felt for Odette or else with the foliage of the Bois where he once heard it (I, 236, 533). The individual, subjective associations are here only to be transcended in the direction of

Essence; even Swann foresees that the delight of art, "instead of being purely individual like that of love," refers to a "superior reality." But essence, in turn, is no longer the stable essence, the seen ideality that unites the world into a whole and introduces the perfect mean into it. Essence, according to Proust, as we have tried to show above, is not something seen but a kind of superior *viewpoint*, an irreducible viewpoint that signifies at once the birth of the world and the original character of a world. It is in this sense that the work of art always constitutes and reconstitutes the beginning of the world, but also forms a specific world absolutely different from the others and envelops a landscape or immaterial site quite distinct from the site where we have grasped it (I, 352; II, 249; III, 895–96). Doubtless it is this aesthetic of the point of view that relates Proust to Henry James. But the important thing is that the viewpoint transcends the individual no less than the essence transcends the mood, the state of soul; the viewpoint remains superior to the person who assumes it or guarantees the identity of all those who attain it. It is not individual, but on the contrary a principle of individuation. This is precisely the originality of Proustian reminiscence: it proceeds from a mood, from a state of soul, and from its associative chains, to a creative or transcendent viewpoint—and no longer, in Plato's fashion, from a state of the world to seen objectivities.

Thus the entire problem of objectivity, like that of unity, is displaced in what we must call a "modern" fashion, essential to modern literature. Order has collapsed, as much in the states of the world that were supposed to reproduce it as in the essences or Ideas that were supposed to inspire it. The world has become crumbs and chaos. Precisely because reminiscence proceeds from subjective associations to an originating viewpoint, objectivity can no longer exist except in the work of art; it no longer exists in significant content as states of the world, nor in ideal signification as stable essence, but solely in the signifying formal structure of the work, in its style. It is no longer a matter of saying: to create is to remember — but rather, to remember is to create, is *to reach that point where the associative chain breaks, leaps over the constituted individual, is transferred to the birth of an individuating world.* And it is no longer a matter of saying: to create is to think — but rather, to think is to create and primarily to create the act of thinking within thought. To think, then, is to provide food for thought. To remember is to create, not to create memory, but to create the spiritual equivalent of the still too material memory, to create the viewpoint valid for all associations, the style valid for all images. It is style that substitutes for experience the manner in which we speak about it or the formula that expresses it, which substitutes for the individual in the world the viewpoint toward a world, and which transforms reminiscence into a realized creation.

The signs are to be found in the Greek world: the great Platonic trilogy — *Phaedrus, Symposium, Phaedo* — of madness, love, and death. The Greek world is expressed not only in the Logos as totality, but in fragments and shreds as objects of aphorisms, in symbols as fractions, in the signs of the oracles, and in the madness or delirium of the soothsayers. But the Greek soul has always had the impression that signs, the mute language of things, were a mutilated system, variable and deceptive, debris of a Logos that was to be restored in a dialectic, reconciled by a *philia*, harmonized by a *sophia*, governed by an Intelligence that comes before. The melancholy of the finest Greek statues is the presentiment that the Logos that animates them will be broken into fragments. Instead of the signs of the fire that herald victory to Clytemnestra — a deceptive and fragmentary language suitable for women — the coryphaeus offers another language, the logos of the messenger that gathers up All into One according to the perfect mean, happiness, and truth.[5] In the language of signs, on the contrary, there is no truth except in what is done in order to deceive, in the meanders of what conceals the truth, in the fragments of a deception and a disaster; there is no truth except a betrayed truth, which is both surrendered by the enemy and revealed by oblique views or by fragments. As in Spinoza's definition of prophecy, the Hebrew prophet deprived of the Logos, reduced to the language of signs, always needs a sign to be convinced that the sign of God is not deceptive. For even God may choose to deceive him.

When a part is valid for itself, when a fragment speaks in itself, when a sign appears, it may be in two very different fashions: either because it permits us to divine the whole from which it is taken, to reconstitute the organism or the statue to which it belongs, and to seek out the other part that belongs to it — or else, on the contrary, because there is no other part that corresponds to it, no totality into which it can enter, no unity from which it is torn and to which it can be restored. The first fashion is that of the Greeks; it is only in this form that they tolerate "aphorisms." The smallest part must still be a *microcosm* for them to recognize in it an adherence to the greater whole of a *macrocosm*. The signs are composed according to analogies and articulations that form a great Organism, as we still find it in the Platonism of the Middle Ages and the Renaissance. They are caught up in an order of the world, in a network of significant contents and ideal significations that still testify to a Logos at the very moment that they break it. And we cannot invoke the fragments of the pre-Socratics in order to turn them into the Jews of Plato; we cannot transform into an intention the fragmented state to which time has reduced their work. Quite the contrary is a work whose object, or rather whose subject, is Time. It concerns, it brings with it fragments that can no longer be restored, pieces that do not fit into the same puzzle, that do not belong to a preceding totality, that do not emanate from the same lost unity. Perhaps that is what time is: the ultimate existence of parts of different sizes and shapes, which cannot be adapted, which do not develop at the same rhythm, and which the stream of style does not sweep along at the same speed. The order of the cosmos has collapsed, crumbled into associative chains and noncommunicating viewpoints. The language of signs begins to speak for itself, reduced to the resources of disaster and deception; it no longer is supported on a subsisting Logos: only the formal structure of the work of art will be capable of deciphering the fragmentary raw material it utilizes, without external reference, without an allegorical or analogical "grid." When Proust seeks precursors in reminiscence, he cites Baudelaire but reproaches him with having made too "voluntary" a use of the method, that is, with having sought objective articulations and analogies that are still too Platonic in a world inhabited by the Logos. What he prefers in Chateaubriand's sentence is that the odor of heliotrope is brought not "by a breeze of one's native land, but by a wild wind of the New World, *without relation to the exiled plant, without sympathy for reminiscence and of voluptuousness*" (Chateaubriand, III, 920). By which we are to understand that there is no Platonic reminiscence here, precisely because there is no sympathy as a reuniting into a whole; rather the messenger is itself an incongruous part that does not correspond to its message nor to the recipient of that message. This is always the case in Proust, and this is his entirely new or modern conception of reminiscence: *an associative, incongruous chain is unified only by a creative viewpoint that itself takes the role of an incongruous part within the whole*. This is the method that guarantees the purity of the encounter or of chance and represses the intelligence, preventing it from "coming before." One would look in vain in Proust for platitudes about the work of art as organic totality in which each part predetermines the whole and in which the whole determines the part (a dialectic conception of the work of art). Even the painting by Vermeer is not valid as a Whole because of the patch of yellow wall planted there as a fragment of still another world (III, 186–87). In the same way, the little phrase of Vinteuil, "interspersed, episodic," about which Odette says to Swann, "Why do you need the rest? Just that is *our* piece" (I, 218–19). And the Balbec church, disappointing as long as we look in it for "an almost Persian impulse" in its entirety, reveals on the contrary its beauty in one of its discordant parts that represents, as a matter of fact, "quasi-Chinese dragons" (I, 841–42). The dragons of Balbec, the patch of wall in the Vermeer, the little phrase of Vinteuil, mysterious viewpoints, tell us the same thing as Chateaubriand's wind: they function without "sympathy," they do not make the work into an organic totality, but rather each acts as a fragment that determines a crystallization. As we shall see, it is no accident that the model of the vegetal in Proust has replaced that of animal totality, as much in the case of art as in that of sexuality. Such a work, having for subject time itself, has no need to write by aphorisms: it is in the meanders and rings of an anti-Logos style that it makes the requisite detours in order to gather up the ultimate fragments, to sweep along at different speeds all the pieces, each one of which refers to a different whole, to no whole at all, or to no other whole than that of style.

CHAPTER 9

Cells and Vessels

To claim that Proust had the notion — even vague or confused — of the antecedent unity of the Search or that he found it subsequently, but as animating the whole from the start, is to read him badly, applying the ready-made criteria of organic totality that are precisely the ones he rejects and missing the new conception of unity he was in the process of creating. For it is surely from here that we must begin: the disparity, the incommensurability, the disintegration of the parts of the Search, with the breaks, lacunae, intermittences that guarantee its ultimate diversity. In this respect, there are two fundamental figures: the one concerns more particularly the relations of container and content, the other the relations of parts and whole. The first is a figure that *encases, envelops, implies*; things, persons, and names are boxes out of which we take something of an entirely different shape, of an entirely different nature, an excessive content. "I tried to remember exactly the line of the roof, the hue of the stone that, without my being able to understand why, had seemed to me full, ready to burst open, to yield me what they merely enclosed . . . (I, 178–79). The voice of M. de Charlus, "that motley character, pot-bellied and closed, like some box of exotic and suspect origin," contains broods of young girls and tutelary feminine souls (II, 1042). Proper names are half-open cases that project their qualities upon the beings they designate: "The name Guermantes is also like one of those tiny balloons in which oxygen or some other gas has been stored" or else like one of those "little tubes" from which we "squeeze" the right color (II, 11–12). And in relation to this first figure of envelopment, the narrator's activity consists in *explicating*, that is, in unfolding, developing a content incommensurable with the container. The second figure is instead that of *complication*; this time it involves the coexistence of asymmetric and noncommunicating parts, either because they are organized as quite separate halves or because they are oriented as opposing "aspects" or ways or because they begin to revolve, to whirl like a lottery wheel that shifts and even mixes the fixed prizes. The narrator's activity then consists in *electing*, in *choosing*; at least this is his apparent activity, for many various forces, themselves complicated within him, are at work to determine his pseudo-will, to make him select a certain part of the complex composition, a certain aspect of the unstable opposition, a certain prize in the circling shadows.

The first figure is dominated by the image of the open boxes, the second by that of the closed vessels. *The first (container/content) is valid with regard to the position of a content without common measure, the second (part/whole) with regard to the opposition of a proximity without communication.* They undoubtedly commingle regularly, shift from one to the other. For instance, Albertine has both aspects; on the one hand, she *complicates* many characters in herself, many girls of whom it seems that each is seen by means of a different optical instrument that must be selected according to the circumstances and nuances of desire; on the other hand, she *implicates* or envelops the beach and the waves, she holds together "all the impressions of a maritime series" that must be unfolded and developed as one might uncoil a cable (II, 362–63). But each of the great categories of the Search nonetheless marks a preference, a commitment to one or the other figure, even in its way of participating secondarily in the one from which it does not originate. This is in fact why we can conceive each great category in one of the two figures, as having its double in the other, and perhaps already inspired by this double that is at once the same and altogether different. Consider language: proper names have first of all their entire power as boxes from which we extract the contents, and, once emptied by disappointment, they are still organized in terms of each other by "enclosing," "imprisoning" all history; but common nouns acquire their value by introducing into discourse certain noncommunicating fragments of truth and lies chosen by the interpreter. Or again, consider the faculties: the particular function of involuntary memory is to open boxes, to deploy a hidden content, while at the other pole, desire, or better still sleep, revolves the sealed vessels, the circular aspects, and chooses the one that best suits a certain depth of sleep, a certain proximity of wakening, a certain degree of love. Or consider love itself: desire and memory combine in order to form precipitates of jealousy, but the former is first of all concerned with multiplying the noncommunicating Albertines, the latter with extracting from Albertine incommensurable "regions of memory."

Thus we may consider abstractly each of the two figures, even if only in order to determine its specific diversity. First of all we shall ask what is the container and of what does the content specifically consist, what is the relation between them, what the form of the "explication," what difficulties it encounters by reason of the container's resistance or the escape of the content, and above all where the incommensurability of the two intervenes, in terms of opposition, hiatus, severance, and so on. In the example of the madeleine, Proust invokes the little pieces of Japanese paper that, under water, swell and unfold, *explicate*: "In the same way now all the flowers of our garden and those of M. Swann, and the water lilies of the Vivonne, and the good souls of the village and their little houses and the church and all Combray and its environs, all that which assumes shape and solidity, has emerged, town and gardens, from my cup of tea" (I, 47). But this is only approximately true. The true container is not the cup, but the sensuous quality, the flavor. And the content is not a chain associated with this flavor, the chain of things and people who were known in Combray, but Combray as essence, Combray as pure Viewpoint, superior to all that has been experienced *from* this viewpoint itself, appearing finally for itself and in its splendor, in a relation of severance with the associative chain that merely came half the way toward it.[1] The content is so completely lost, having never been possessed, that its reconquest is a creation. And it is precisely because Essence as individuating viewpoint surmounts the entire chain of individual association with which it breaks that it has the power not simply to remind us, however intensely, of the self that has experienced the entire chain, but to make that self relive, by reindividuating it, a pure existence that it has never experienced. Every "explication" of something, in this sense, is the resurrection of a self.

The beloved is like the sensuous quality, valid by what she envelops. Her eyes would be merely stones, and her body a piece of flesh, if they did not express a possible world or worlds, landscapes and places, ways of life that must be explicated—unfolded, uncoiled like the bits of Japanese paper: thus, Mlle de Stermaria and Brittany, Albertine, and Balbec. Love and jealousy are strictly governed by this activity of explication. There is even something of a double movement by which a landscape requires to be wrapped within a woman, as the woman must unwrap the landscapes and places she "contains" enclosed within her body (I, 156–57). Expressivity is the content of another person. And here too we might suppose that there is merely a relation of association between content and container. Yet, although the associative chain is strictly necessary, there is something more, something that Proust defines as the indivisible character of desire that seeks to give a form to matter and to fill form with matter.[2] But again, that the chain of associations exists only in relation with a force that will break it, is shown by a curious torsion by which we are ourselves caught in the unknown world expressed by the beloved, emptied of ourselves, taken up into this other universe (I, 716; I, 794). So that to be seen produces the same effect as to hear one's name spoken by the beloved: the effect of being held, naked, in her mouth (I, 401). The association of a landscape and the beloved in the narrator's mind is therefore dissolved—the beloved's viewpoint takes supremacy over the landscape, a supremacy in which the narrator himself is involved, even

if only by his exclusion from it. But this time the breaking of the associative chain is not transcended by the appearance of an Essence; instead it results in an emptying
operation that restores the narrator to himself. For the
narrator-interpreter, loving and jealous, will imprison the
beloved, immure her, sequester her in order to "explicate" her, that is, to empty her of all the worlds she contains. "By imprisoning Albertine, I had thereby restored
all those iridescent wings to the world. . . . They constituted
its beauty. They had once constituted Albertine's. . . . Albertine had lost all her colors . . . she had gradually lost all
her beauty. . . . Having become the gray captive, reduced
to her own term, it required those flashes in which I re-
membered the past in order to restore those colors to her"
(III, 172–73). And only jealousy momentarily re-engrosses
her with a universe that a gradual explication will seek to
empty in its turn. To restore the narrator to himself? Ultimately something quite different is involved: emptying
each of the selves that loved Albertine, bringing each to
its term according to a law of death intertwined with the
law of resurrection, as Time lost is intertwined with Time
regained. And such selves are just as eager to seek their
own suicide, to repeat/prepare their own end, as to come
to life again as something else, to repeat/remember their
life.[3]

Names themselves have a content inseparable from
the qualities of their syllables and from the free associations in which they participate. But precisely because we
cannot open the box without projecting this entire associated content upon the real person or place, conversely,
obligatory and entirely different associations imposed by

the mediocrity of the person or the place will distort and dissolve the first series and create, this time, a gap between content and container.[4] In all the aspects of this first figure of the Search, then, the inadequation, the incommensurability of the content is manifested: *it is either a lost content*, which we regain in the splendor of an essence resuscitating an earlier self, *or an emptied content*, which brings the self to its death, *or a separated content*, which casts us into an inevitable disappointment. A world can never be organized hierarchically and objectively, and even the subjective chains of association that give it a minimum of consistency or order break down, to the advantage of transcendent but variable and violently imbricated viewpoints, some expressing truths of absence and time lost, others the truths of presence or of time regained. Names, persons, and things are crammed with a content that fills them to bursting; and not only are we present at this "dynamiting" of the containers by the contents, but at the explosion of the contents themselves that, unfolded, explicated, do not form a unique figure, but heterogeneous, fragmented truths still more in conflict among themselves than in agreement. Even when the past is given back to us in essences, the pairing of the present moment and the past one is more like a struggle than an agreement, and what is given us is neither a totality nor an eternity, but "a bit of time in the pure state," that is, a fragment (III, 705). Nothing is ever pacified by a *philia*; as in the case of places and moments, two emotions that unite do so only by struggling, and form in this struggle an irregular short-lived body. Even in the highest state of essence as artistic Viewpoint, the world that begins emits sounds in conflict like the ultimate disparate fragments on which it is based. "Soon the two motifs struggled together in a hand-to-hand combat in which sometimes one vanished altogether, in which then one perceived no more than a fragment of the other."

It is doubtless this that accounts for that extraordinary energy of unmatched parts in the Search, whose rhythms of deployment or rates of explication are irreducible; not only do they not compose a whole together, but they do not testify separately to a whole from which each part is torn, different from every other, in a kind of dialogue between universes. But the force with which the parts are projected into the world, violently stuck together despite their unmatching edges, causes them to be recognized as parts, though without composing a whole, even a hidden one, without emanating from totalities, even lost ones. By setting fragments into fragments, Proust finds the means of making us contemplate them all, but without reference to a unity from which they might derive or which itself would derive from them.[5]

As for the second figure of the Search, the complication that concerns, more particularly, the relation between parts and whole, we see that it too applies to words, to persons and to things, that is, to moments and places. *The image of the sealed vessel, which marks the opposition of one part to uncorresponding environs, here replaces the image of the open box, which marked the position of a content incommensurable with the container.* Thus the two ways of the Search, the Méséglise Way and the Guermantes Way, remain juxtaposed, "unknowable to each other, in sealed vessels and without communication between them of different afternoons" (I, 135). It is impossible to do what Gilberte says: "We could go to Guermantes by the Méséglise way." Even the final revelation of time regained will not unify them nor make them converge, but will multiply the "transversals" that themselves are not interconnected (III, 1029). Similarly, the faces of others have at least two dissymmetric sides, like "two opposing routes that will never meet": thus for Rachel, the way of generality and that of singularity, or else that of the shapeless nebula seen from too close and that of an exquisite organization from the right distance. Or else for Albertine, the face that corresponds to trust and the face that reacts to jealous suspicion (III, 489; II, 159, 174–75), and again the two routes or the two ways are only statistical directions. We can form a complex group, but we never form it *without its splitting in its turn, this time as though into a thousand sealed vessels*: thus Albertine's face, when we imagine we are gathering it up in itself for a kiss, leaps from one plane to another as our lips cross its cheek, "ten Albertines" in sealed vessels, until the final moment when everything disintegrates in the exaggerated proximity.[6] And in each vessel is a self that lives, perceives, desires, and remembers, that wakes or sleeps, that dies, commits suicide, and revives in abrupt jolts: the "crumbling," the "fragmentation" of Albertine to which corresponds a multiplication of the self. The same piece of information taken as a whole, Albertine's departure, must be learned by all these distinct selves, each at the bottom of its urn (III, 430).

At another level, is this not the case of the world, a statistical reality within which "the worlds" are as separated as infinitely distant stars, each having its signs and its hierarchies that function so that a Swann or a Charlus will never be recognized by the Verdurins, until the great mixture of the end whose new laws the narrator renounces trying to learn, as if he had here too attained that threshold of proximity at which everything disintegrates and again becomes nebulous? In the same way, finally, utterance in general effects a statistical distribution of *words*, in which the interpreter discerns layers, families, allegiances, and borrowings that are very different from each other, that testify to the links of the speaker, to his frequentations and his secret worlds, as if each world belonged to a specifically tinted aquarium, containing a certain species of fish, beyond the pseudo-unity of the Logos: thus certain words that did not constitute part of Albertine's earlier vocabulary and that persuade the narrator that she has become more approachable by entering a new age-class and new relationships, or again the dreadful expression "get yourself done in" that reveals to the narrator a whole world of abomination (II, 354–55; III, 337–41). And this is why the lie belongs to the language of signs, unlike the logos-truth: according to the image of unmatching puzzle-pieces, words themselves are world-fragments that should correspond to other fragments of the same world, but not to other fragments of other worlds with which they are nonetheless brought into proximity.[7] Thus there is in words a kind of geographical and linguistic basis for the psychology of the liar.

This is what the closed vessels signify: there is no totality except a statistical one that lacks any profound meaning. "What we suppose our love or our jealousy to be is not a single continuous indivisible passion, but an infinity of successive loves, of different jealousies, which are ephemeral, but by their uninterrupted multitude give the impression of continuity, the illusion of unity" (I, 371–73). Yet among all these sealed vessels, there exists a system of communication, though it must not be confused with a direct means of access, nor with a means of totalization. As between the Méséglise Way and the Guermantes Way, the entire work consists in establishing *transversals* that cause us to leap from one of Albertine's profiles to the other, from one Albertine to another, from one world to another, from one word to another, without ever reducing the many to the One, without ever gathering up the multiple into a whole, but affirming the original unity of precisely that multiplicity, affirming without uniting *all* these irreducible fragments. Jealousy is the transversal of love's multiplicity; travel, the transversal of the multiplicity of places; sleep, the transversal of the multiplicity of moments. The sealed vessels are sometimes organized in separate parts, sometimes in opposing directions, sometimes (as in certain journeys or as in sleep) in a circle. But it is striking that even the circle does not surround, does not totalize, but makes detours and loops, so that it shifts what was on the left to the right, bypasses what was previously in the center. And the unity of all the views of a train journey is not established on the basis of the circle itself (whose parts remain sealed), nor on the basis of the thing contemplated, but on a transversal that we never cease to follow, moving "from one window to the next."[8]

For travel does not connect places, but affirms only their difference.[9]

The narrator's activity no longer consists in explicating, unfolding a content, but in choosing a noncommunicating part, a sealed vessel, with the self that occurs within it. To choose a certain girl in the group, a certain view or fixed notion of the girl, to choose a certain word in what she says, a certain suffering in what we feel for her, and, in order to experience this suffering, in order to decipher the word, in order to love this girl, to choose a certain self that we cause to live or relive among all the possible selves: such is the activity corresponding to complication.[10] This activity of choice, in its purest form, is performed at the moment of waking, when sleep has made all the sealed vessels revolve, all the closed rooms, all the isolated selves haunted by the sleeper. Not only are there the different rooms of sleep that circle the insomniac about to choose his drug ("sleep of the datura, of Indian hemp, of the various extracts of ether...")—but every sleeper "holds in a circle around him the thread of the hours, the order of the years and worlds": the problem of awakening is to leave this room of sleep, and of what unfolds there, for the real room in which one is; to rediscover the previous day's self among all those we have just been in our dreams, which we might be or have been; to rediscover, finally, the chain of associations that links us to reality by leaving the superior viewpoints of sleep.[11] We shall not ask *who* chooses. Certainly no self, because we ourselves are chosen, because a certain self is chosen each time that "we" choose a person to love, a suffering to experience, and each time this self is no less surprised to live or to relive, and to answer the call, whatever the delay. Thus emerging from sleep, "we are no longer anyone. How, then, seeking our mind, our personality, as we seek a lost object, do we end by regaining our own self rather than any other? Why, when we begin thinking again, is it not another personality than the previous one that is incarnated in us? We do not see what it is that dictates the choice and why, among the millions of human beings we might be, it is precisely the one we were the day before that we become again" (II, 88). Indeed, there exists an activity, a pure *interpreting*, a pure choosing that has no more subject than it has object, because it chooses the interpreter no less than the thing to interpret, the sign and the self that deciphers it. Such is the "we" of interpretation: "But we do not even say *we*...a we that would be without content" (II, 981). It is in this that sleep is profounder than memory, for memory—even involuntary memory—remains attached to the sign that solicits it and to the already chosen self that it will revive, whereas sleep is the image of that pure *interpreting* that is involved in every sign and develops in every faculty. Interpreting has no other unity than a transversal one; interpreting alone is the divinity of which each thing is a fragment, but its "divine form" neither collects nor unites the fragments, it carries them on the contrary to the highest, most acute state, preventing them from forming a whole. The "subject" of the Search is finally no self, it is that *we* without content that portions out Swann, the narrator, and Charlus, distributes or selects them without totalizing them.

We have previously found signs distinguished by their objective substance, their subjective chain of association, the faculty that deciphers them, their relation with essence. But, formally, the signs are of two types that we encounter in all the various kinds: those open boxes, which are to be explicated; those sealed vessels, which are to be chosen. And if the sign is always a fragment without totalization or unification, this is because content relates to container by all the power of its incommensurability, just as the sealed vessel relates to its environs by all the power of its noncommunication. Incommensurability and noncommunication are distances, but distances that fit together or intersect. And this is precisely what time signifies: that system of nonspatial distances, that distance proper to the contiguous or to the continuous, *distances without intervals*. In this regard, lost time, which introduces distances between contiguous things, and time regained, which on the contrary establishes a contiguity of distant things, function in a complementary manner depending on whether it is forgetting or memory that effect "irregular, fragmented interpolations." For the difference between lost time and time regained is not yet here; and the former, by its power of sickness, age, and forgetting, affirms the fragments as disjunct no less than the latter, by its power of memory and resurrection.[12] In any case, according to the Bergsonian formula, time signifies that everything is not given; the Whole is not givable. This means not that the whole "is created" in another dimension that would be, precisely, temporal, as Bergson understands it or as it is understood by the partisan dialecticians of a totalizing process. But because time, ultimate interpreter, ultimate act of interpretation, has the strange power to affirm simultaneously fragments that do not constitute a whole in space, any more than they form a whole by succession within time. Time is precisely the transversal of all possible spaces, including the space of time.

CHAPTER 10

Levels of the Search

In a universe thus fragmented, there is no Logos that gathers up all the pieces, hence no law attaches them to a whole to be regained or even formed. And yet there is a law, but with a changed nature, function, and relation. The Greek world is a world in which the law is always secondary; it is a secondary power in relation to the logos that comprehends the whole and refers it to the Good. The law, or rather the laws, merely control the parts, adapt them, bring them together and unite them, establish in them a relative "better." Thus the laws are valid only to the degree that they cause us to know something of what transcends them and to the degree that they determine an image of the "better," meaning the aspect assumed by the Good in the logos in relation to certain parts, a certain region, a certain moment. It seems that the modern consciousness of the antilogos has made the law undergo a radical revolution. The law becomes a primary power insofar as it controls a world of untotalizable and untotalized fragments. The law no longer says what is good, but good is what the law says; it thereby acquires a formidable unity: there are no longer laws specified in such and such a manner, but there is *the* law, without any other specification. It is true that this formidable unity is absolutely empty, uniquely formal, because it causes us to know no distinct object, no totality, no Good of reference, no referring Logos. Far from conjoining and adapting parts, it separates and partitions them, sets noncommunication in the contiguous, incommensurability in the container. Not causing us to know anything, the law teaches us what it is only by marking our flesh, by already applying punishment to us, and thus the fantastic paradox: we do not know what the law intended before receiving punishment, hence we can obey the law only by being guilty, we can be answerable to it only by our guilt, because the law is applied to parts only as disjunct, and by disjoining them still further, by dismembering bodies, by tearing their members from them. Strictly speaking unknowable, the law makes itself known only by applying the harshest punishments to our agonized body.

Modern consciousness of the law assumed a particularly acute form with Kafka: it is in *The Great Wall of China* that we find the fundamental link between the fragmentary character of the wall, the fragmentary mode of its construction, and the unknowable character of the law, its determination identical to a punishment of guilt. In Proust, however, the law presents another figure, because guilt is more like the appearance that conceals a more profound fragmentary reality, instead of being itself this more profound reality to which the detached fragments lead us. The depressive consciousness of the law as it appears in Kafka is countered in this sense by the schizoid consciousness of the law according to Proust. At first glance, however, guilt plays a large part in Proust's work, with its essential object: homosexuality. To love supposes the guilt of the beloved, although all love is dispute over evidence, a judgment of innocence rendered upon the being one knows nonetheless to be guilty. Love is therefore a declaration of imaginary innocence extended between two certitudes of guilt, one that conditions love a priori and makes it possible, and one that seals off love, which marks its experimental conclusion. Thus the narrator cannot love Albertine without having grasped this a priori guilt, which he will spin off into all his experience through his conviction that she is innocent in spite of everything (this conviction being quite necessary, functioning as a revealing-agent): "Moreover, even more than their faults while we love them, there are their faults before we knew them, and first among them all: their nature. What makes such loves painful, as a matter of fact, is that they are preexisted by a kind of original sin of women, a sin that makes us love them..." (III, 150–51). "Was it not, in fact, despite all the denials of my reason, to know Albertine in all her hideousness, to choose her, to love her?... To feel ourselves drawn toward such a being, to begin to love her, however innocent we claimed her to be, is to read already, in a different version, all that being's betrayals and faults" (III, 611). And love ends when the a priori certitude of guilt has itself completed its trajectory, when it has become empirical, driving out the empirical conviction that Albertine was innocent in spite of everything: an idea "gradually forming in the depths of consciousness replaced there the idea that Albertine was innocent: this was the idea that she was guilty," so that the certitude of Albertine's sins appears to the narrator only when they no longer interest him, when he has stopped loving, conquered by fatigue and habit (III, 535).

With all the more reason, guilt appears in the two homosexual series. And we recall the power with which

Proust characterizes male homosexuality as accursed, "a race anathematized, and which must live in deception... whose honor is always precarious, whose freedom is always provisional, whose situation is always unstable": homosexuality-as-sign as opposed to the Greek version, homosexuality-as-logos.[1] *Yet the reader has the impression that this guilt is more apparent than real;* and if Proust himself speaks of the originality of his project, if he declares that he himself has tested several "theories," this is because he is not content to isolate specifically an accursed homosexuality. The entire theme of the accursed or guilty race is intertwined, moreover, with a theme of innocence, the theme of the sexuality of plants. The Proustian theory is extremely complex because it functions on several levels. *On a first level* is the entity of heterosexual loves in their contrasts and repetitions. *On a second level,* this entity splits into two series or directions, that of Gomorrah, which conceals the (invariably revealed) secret of the loved woman, and that of Sodom, which carries the still more deeply buried secret of the lover. It is on this level that the idea of sin or guilt prevails. But this second level is not the most profound, because it is no less statistical than the entity it decomposes: in this sense, guilt is experienced socially rather than morally or internally. It will be noticed as a general rule in Proust that not only does a given entity have no more than a statistical value, but also that this is true of the two dissymmetrical aspects or directions into which that entity is divided. For example, the "army" or "throng" of all the narrator's selves that love Albertine forms an entity on the first level, but the two subgroups of "trust" and of "jealous suspicion" are, on a second level, directions that are still statistical, which mask impulses from a third level, the agitations of singular particles, of each of the selves that constitute the throng or army.[2] In the same way, the Méséglise Way and the Guermantes Way are to be taken only as statistical, themselves composed of a host of elementary figures. And in the same way, finally, the Gomorrah and Sodom series, and their corresponding guilts, are doubtless more subtle than the crude appearance of heterosexual loves, but still conceal an ultimate level, constituted by the behavior of organs and of elementary particles.

Even here what interests Proust in the two homosexual series, and what makes them strictly complementary, is the prophecy of separation that they fulfill: "The two sexes shall die, each in a place apart" (III, 616). But the metaphor of the open boxes or the sealed vessels will assume its entire meaning only if we consider that the two sexes are both present and separate in the same individual: contiguous but partitioned and not communicating, in the mystery of an initial hermaphroditism. Here the vegetal theme takes on its full significance, in opposition to a Logos-as-Organism: hermaphroditism is not the property of a now-lost animal totality, but the actual partitioning of the two sexes in one and the same plant: "The male organ is separated by a partition from the female organ" (II, 626, 701). And it is here that *the third level* will be situated: an individual of a given sex (but no sex is given except in the aggregate or statistically) bears within itself the other sex with which it cannot communicate directly. How many young girls lodge within Charlus, and how many who will also become grandmothers! (II, 907, 967).

"In some ... the woman is not only inwardly united with the man, but hideously visible, agitated as by a spasm of hysteria, by a shrill laugh that convulses knees and hands" (II, 620). The first level was defined by the statistical entity of heterosexual loves. The second, by the two homosexual (and still statistical) series, according to which an individual considered within the preceding entity was referred to other individuals of the same sex—participating in the Sodom series if a man, in the Gomorrah series if a woman (hence Odette, Albertine). But the third level is transexual ("which is very wrongly called homosexuality"), and transcends the individual as well as the entity: it designates in the individual the coexistence of fragments of both sexes, *partial objects* that do not communicate. And it will be with them as with plants: the hermaphrodite requires a third party (the insect) so that the female part may be fertilized or the male part may fertilize (II, 602, 626). An aberrant communication occurs in a transversal dimension between partitioned sexes. Or rather, it is even more complicated, for we shall rediscover, on this third level, the distinction of the second and the third levels. It may in fact happen that an individual statistically determined as male will seek, in order to fertilize his female part with which he cannot himself communicate, an individual statistically of the same sex as himself (the same is true for the woman and the male part). But in a more profound instance, the individual statistically determined as male will cause his own female part to be fertilized by objects (themselves partial) that are just as likely to be found in a woman as in a man. And this is the basis of transexuality, according to Proust: no longer an *aggregate and specific homosexuality*, in which men relate to men and women to women in a separation of the two series, but a *local and nonspecific homosexuality*, in which a man also seeks what is masculine in a woman and a woman what is feminine in a man, and this in the partitioned contiguity of the two sexes as partial objects.[3]

Whence the apparently obscure text in which Proust counters an aggregate and specific homosexuality by this local and nonspecific homosexuality: "For some, doubtless those whose childhoods were timid, the material kind of pleasure they take does not matter, so long as they can relate it to a male countenance. While others, whose sensuality is doubtless more violent, give their material pleasure certain imperious localizations. The second group would shock most people by their avowals. They live perhaps less exclusively under Saturn's satellite, for in their case women are not entirely excluded.... But those in the second group seek out women who prefer women, women who suggest young men ... indeed, they can take, with such women, the same pleasure as with a man. Hence those who love members of the first group suffer jealousy only at the thought of pleasure taken with a man—the only kind of pleasure that seems to them a betrayal, because they do not feel love for women and indeed *make love* to them only as a necessity, to preserve the possibility of marriage, being so unconcerned with the pleasure it might afford that they are indifferent if those they love experience it; while those in the second group often inspire jealousy by their love for women. For in their relations with women, they play—for the woman who prefers women—the role of another woman, and at the same time a woman

offers them approximately what they find in a man..."
(II, 622). If we take this transexuality as the ultimate level
of the Proustian theory and its relation with the practice
of partitioning, not only is the vegetal metaphor illumi-
nated but it becomes quite grotesque to wonder about the
degree of "transposition" that Proust had to effect, supposedly, to change an Albert into Albertine, and even more
grotesque to present as a revelation the discovery that
Proust must have had some erotic relationships with
women. One may indeed say that life brings nothing to
the work or theory, for the work or the theory are linked
to the secret life by a link more profound than that of
any biography. It suffices to follow what Proust explains
in his great discussion of Sodom and Gomorrah: transexuality, that is, local and nonspecific homosexuality, based
on the contiguous partitioning of the sexes-as-organs or
of partial objects, which we discover at a deeper level than
aggregate and specific homosexuality, based on the independence of the sexes-as-persons or of entire series.

Jealousy is the very delirium of signs. And, in Proust,
we shall find the confirmation of a fundamental link between jealousy and homosexuality, though it affords an
entirely new interpretation of the latter. Insofar as the
beloved contains possible worlds, it is a matter of explicating, of unfolding all these worlds. But precisely because these worlds are made valid only by the beloved's
viewpoint of them, which is what determines the way in
which they are implicated within the beloved, the lover
can never be sufficiently *involved* in these worlds without
being thereby excluded from them as well, because he belongs to them only as a thing seen, hence also as a thing

scarcely seen, not remarked, excluded from the superior viewpoint from which the choice is made. The gaze of the beloved integrates me within the landscape and the environs only by driving me out of the impenetrable viewpoint according to which the landscape and the environs are organized within the beloved: "If she had seen me, what could I have meant to her? Within what universe did she distinguish me? It would have been as difficult for me to say as, when our telescope shows us certain features of a neighboring planet, it is difficult to conclude from them that human beings inhabit it, that they see us as well, and what ideas their vision might awaken in them" (I, 794). Similarly, the preferences or the caresses the beloved gives me affect me only by suggesting the image of possible worlds in which others have been or are or will be preferred (I, 276). This is why, in the second place, jealousy is no longer simply the explication of *possible worlds* enveloped in the beloved (where others, like myself, can be seen and chosen), but the discovery of the *unknowable world* that represents the beloved's own viewpoint and develops within the beloved's homosexual series. Here the beloved is no longer in relation to anything except beings of the same kind but different from me, sources of pleasures that remain unknown to me and unavailable: "It was a terrible terra incognita in which I had just landed, a new phase of unsuspected sufferings that was beginning" (II, 1115). Lastly, in the third place, jealousy discovers the transexuality of the beloved, everything hidden by the apparent and statistically determined sex of the beloved, the other contiguous and noncommunicating sexes, and the strange insects whose task it is, nonetheless, to bring these aspects into communication — in short, the discovery of partial objects, even more cruel than the discovery of rival persons.

There is a logic of jealousy that is that of the open boxes and sealed vessels. The logic of jealousy comes down to this: to sequester, to immure the beloved. Such is the law Swann divines at the end of his love for Odette, which the narrator already apprehends in his love for his mother, though without yet having the strength to apply it, and which he ultimately applies in his love for Albertine (I, 563; III, 434). The shadowy captives constitute the entire secret filiation of the Search. To sequester is first of all to empty the beloved of all the possible worlds she contains, to decipher and explicate these worlds; but it is also to relate them to the enveloping impulse, to the implication that marks their relation to the beloved (III, 172–74). Next, it is to break off the homosexual series that constitutes the beloved's unknown world and also to discover homosexuality as the beloved's original sin, for which the beloved is punished by being sequestered. Lastly, to sequester is to prevent the contiguous aspects, the sexes, and the partial objects from communicating within the transversal dimension haunted by the insect (the third object); it is to enclose each by itself, thereby interrupting the accursed exchanges, but it is also to set them beside each other and to let them invent their system of communication, which always exceeds our expectations, which creates amazing accidents and outwits our suspicions (the secret of the signs). There is an astonishing relation between the sequestration born of jealousy, the passion to see, and the action of profaning: sequestration, voyeurism, and profanation — the Proustian trinity. For to imprison is, precisely, to put oneself in a position to see without being seen, that is, without the risk of being carried away by the beloved's viewpoint that excluded us from the world as much as it included us within it. Thus, seeing Albertine asleep. To see is indeed to reduce the beloved to the contiguous, noncommunicating aspects that constitute her and to await the transversal mode of communication that these partitioned halves will find the means of instituting. Seeing therefore transcends the temptation of letting others see, even symbolically. To make another person see is to impose on him the contiguity of a strange, abominable, hideous spectacle. It not only imposes on him the vision of the sealed and contiguous vessels, partial objects between which a coupling *contra naturam* is suggested, but treats that person as if he were one of these objects, one of these contiguous aspects that must communicate transversally.

Whence the theme of profanation so dear to Proust. Mlle Vinteuil associates her father's photograph with her sexual revels. The narrator puts family furniture in a brothel. By making Albertine embrace him next to his mother's room, he can reduce his mother to the state of a partial object (tongue) contiguous to Albertine's body. Or else, in a dream, he cages his parents like wounded mice at the mercy of the transversal movements that penetrate them and make them jump. Everywhere, to profane is to make the mother (or the father) function as a partial object, that is, to partition her, to make her see a contiguous spectacle, and even to participate in this spectacle she can no longer interrupt and no longer leave—to make her contiguous to the spectacle.[4]

Freud assigned two fundamental anxieties in relation to the law: aggression against the beloved involves, on the one hand, a threat of the loss of love, and on the other, a guilt caused by turning that aggression against the self. The second figure gives the law a depressive conscious-ness, but the first one represents a schizoid consciousness of the law. Now, in Proust the theme of guilt remains su-perficial, social rather than moral, projected upon others rather than internalized in the narrator, distributed within the various statistical series. On the other hand, the loss of love truly defines destiny or the law: *to love without being loved*, because love implicates the seizure of these possi-ble worlds in the beloved, worlds that expel me as much as they draw me in and that culminate in the unknowable homosexual world—but also *to stop loving*, because the emptying of the worlds, the explication of the beloved, lead the self that loves to its death.[5] "To be harsh and decep-tive to what one loves," because it is a matter of seques-tering the beloved, of seeing the beloved when she can no longer see you, then of making her see the partitioned scenes of which she is the shameful theater or simply the horrified spectator. To sequester, to see, to profane—sum-marizes the entire law of love.

This is to say that law in general, in a world devoid of the logos, controls the parts without a whole whose open or sealed nature we have examined. And far from uniting or gathering them together in the same world, the law measures their discrepancy, their remoteness, their distance, and their partitioning, establishing only aberrant communications between the noncommunicating vessels, transversal unities between the boxes that resist any totalization, inserting by force into one world the fragment of another world, propelling the diverse worlds and viewpoints into the infinite void of distances. This is why, on its simplest level, the law as social or natural law appears in terms of the telescope, not the microscope. Of course Proust borrows the vocabulary of the infinitely small: Albertine's various faces differ by "a deviation of infinitesimal lines" (II, 366; I, 945–46). But even here, the tiny deviations of lines are significant only as bearers of colors that separate and diverge from each other, modifying the dimensions of the faces. The instrument of the Search is the telescope, not the microscope, because infinite distances always subtend infinitesimal attractions and because the theme of telescoping unites the three Proustian figures of what is seen from a distance, the collision between worlds, and the folding-up of parts one within another. "Soon I was able to show some sketches. No one could make anything out of them. Even those who favored my perception of the truths I later tried to engrave in time congratulated me on having discovered them by 'microscope,' when I had, on the contrary, made use of a telescope in order to perceive things — tiny, indeed, but tiny because they were situated at a great distance, and each of which constituted a world. Though I was in search of great laws, I was labeled a hair-splitter, a rummager among details" (III, 1041). The restaurant dining room includes as many planets as there are tables around which the waiters revolve; the group of girls executes apparently irregular movements whose laws can be discerned only by patient observation, "impassioned astronomy"; the world enveloped within Albertine has the particularities of what appears to us in a planet, "thanks to the telescope" (I, 794, 810, 831). And if suffering is a sun, it is because its rays immediately traverse distances without annulling them. This is precisely what we have observed in the case of the partitioning of contiguous things: contiguity does not reduce distance to the infinitesimal but affirms and even extends a distance without interval, according to an ever astronomical, ever telescopic law that governs the fragments of disparate universes.

CHAPTER 11

The Three Machines

And the telescope functions. A psychic telescope for an "impassioned astronomy," the Search is not merely an instrument Proust uses at the same time that he fabricates it. It is an instrument for others and whose use others must learn: "They would not be my readers, but the proper readers of themselves, my book being merely a kind of magnifying glass like the ones shown to the prospective buyer by the optician of Combray — my book, thanks to which I supplied them the means of reading within themselves. So that I would not ask them to praise me or to denigrate me, but merely to tell me if this is the case, if the words that they read in themselves are indeed the ones I have written (the possible divergences in this regard not necessarily resulting in every case, moreover, from the fact that I have been wrong, but occasionally from the fact that the reader's eyes are not those that my book would suit in order to read accurately in himself)."[1] And the Search is not only an instrument, but a machine. The modern work of art is anything it may seem; it is even its very property of being whatever we like, of having the overdetermination of whatever we like, from the moment *it works*: the modern work of art is a machine and functions as such. Malcolm Lowry says, splendidly, of his novel: "It can be regarded as a kind of symphony, or in another way as a kind of opera — or even a horse opera. It is hot music, a poem, a song, a tragedy, a comedy, a farce, and so forth. It is superficial, profound, entertaining and boring, according to taste. It is a prophecy, a political warning, a cryptogram, a preposterous movie, and a writing on the wall. It can even be regarded as a sort of machine: it works too, believe me, as I have found out."[2] Proust means nothing else by advising us not to read his work but to make use of it in order to read within ourselves. There is not a sonata or a septet in the Search; it is the Search that is a sonata and a septet as well, and also an opera buffa, and even, Proust adds, a cathedral and also a gown (III, 1033). And it is a prophecy about the sexes, a political warning that reaches us from the depths of the Dreyfus Affair and the First World War, a cryptogram that decodes and recodes all our social, diplomatic, strategic, erotic, and aesthetic languages, a western or a wacky comedy about the Captive, writing on the wall and salon guide, a metaphysical treatise, a delirium of signs or of jealousy, an exercise in training the faculties; anything we like provided we make the whole thing work, and "it works, believe me." To the *logos*, organ and organon whose meaning must be discovered in the whole to which it belongs, is opposed the antilogos, machine and machinery whose meaning (anything you like) depends solely on its functioning, which, in turn, depends on its separate parts. The modern work of art has no problem of meaning, it has only a problem of use.

Why a machine? Because the work of art, so understood, is essentially productive—productive of certain truths. No one has insisted more than Proust on the following point: that the truth is produced, that it is produced by orders of machines that function within us, that it is extracted from our impressions, hewn out of our life, delivered in a work. This is why Proust rejects so forcefully the state of a truth that is not produced but merely discovered or, on the contrary, created, and the state of a thought that would presuppose itself by putting intelligence "before," uniting all one's faculties in a voluntary use corresponding to discovery or to creation (Logos). "The ideas formed by pure intelligence have only a *logical* or possible truth, their choice is arbitrary. The book with letters figured, not drawn by us, is our only book. Not that the ideas we form cannot be accurate *logically*, but we do not know if they are true." And the creative imagination is worth no more than the discovering or observing intelligence.[3]

We have seen how Proust revived the Platonic equivalence of creating/remembering. But this is because memory and creation are no more than two aspects of the same production — "interpreting," "deciphering," and "translating" being here the process of production itself. It is because the work of art is a form of production that it does not raise a special problem of meaning, but rather of use.[4] Even the activity of thinking must be produced within thought. All production starts from the impression because only the impression unites in itself the accident of the encounter and the necessity of the effect, a violence that it obliges us to undergo. Thus all production starts from a sign and supposes the depth and darkness of the involuntary. "Imagination and thought can be splendid machines in themselves, but they can be inert; it is suffering that then sets them in motion" (III, 909). Then, as we have seen, the sign according to its nature awakens one

faculty or another, but never all together, and impels it to
the limit of its involuntary and disjunct exercise by which
it produces meaning. A kind of classification of signs has
shown us the faculties that functioned in one case or another and the kind of meaning produced (notably *general
laws* or *singular essences*). In any case, the chosen faculty
under the sign's constraint constitutes the interpreting action, which produces the meaning, law, or essence according to the case, but always a product. This is because the
meaning (truth) is never in the impression nor even in
the memory, but is identified with "the spiritual equivalent" of the memory or of the impression produced by
the involuntary machine of interpretation.[5] It is this notion of the spiritual equivalent that establishes a new link
between remembering and creating and establishes it in
a process of production as a work of art.

The Search is indeed the production of the sought-
for truth. Again, there is no truth, but orders of truth, just
as there are orders of production. And it is not even enough
to say that there are truths of time regained and truths of
lost time. For the great final systematization distinguishes
not two, but three orders of truth. It is true that the first
order seems to concern time regained because it comprehends all the cases of natural reminiscence and aesthetic
essence, and it is true that the second and third orders
seem to be identified in the flux of lost time and to produce only secondary truths that are said to "enshrine" or
to "cement" those of the first order (III, 898, 932, 967).
Yet the determination of substances and the movement
of the text oblige us to distinguish the three orders. The
first order to appear is defined by reminiscences and

essences, that is, by *singularity*, and by the production of time regained that corresponds to them and the conditions and agents of such production (natural and artistic signs). The second order is just as much concerned with art and the work of art, but it groups the pleasures and pains that are unfulfilled in themselves, which refer to something else, even if this something else and its finality remain unperceived, for example, worldly signs and the signs of love — in short, whatever obeys *general laws* and intervenes in the production of lost time (for lost time, too, is a matter of production). The third order still concerns art, but is defined by *universal* alteration, death and the idea of death, the production of catastrophe (signs of aging, disease, and death). As for the movement of the text, it is in an entirely different way that truths of the second order reinforce those of the first by a kind of analogy, of proof *a contrario* in another domain of production, and that those of the third order doubtless reinforce those of the first while raising a veritable "objection" to these truths that must be "surmounted" between the two orders of production.[6]

The whole problem is in the nature of these three orders of truth. If we do not follow the order of presentation of time regained, which is necessarily given primacy from the viewpoint of the final exposition, we must consider as a primary order the unfulfilled pains and pleasures whose finality is undetermined and obey general laws. Now, curiously, Proust groups here the values of worldliness with their frivolous pleasures, the values of love with their sufferings, and even the values of sleep with their dreams. In the "vocation" of a man of letters, these all constitute an "apprenticeship," meaning the familiarity with a raw material that we will recognize only subsequently in the finished product (III, 899–907). Doubtless these are extremely different signs, notably the worldly signs and the signs of love, but we have seen that their common point lay in the faculty that interpreted them — the intelligence, but an intelligence that "comes after" instead of "coming before," obliged by the constraint of the sign. And it lay in the meaning that corresponds to these signs: always a general law, whether this law is that of a group, as in worldliness, or that of a series of beloved beings, as in love. But this is still no more than a matter of crude resemblances. If we consider this first kind of machine more closely, we see that it is defined chiefly by a production of *partial objects* as they have been previously defined, fragments without totality, vessels without communication, partitioned scenes. Further, if there is always a general law, it is in the particular meaning that the law inheres in Proust, not uniting into a whole, but on the contrary covering distances, separations, partitionings. If dreams appear in this group, it is by their capacity to telescope fragments, to set different universes in motion, and to cross, without annulling, "enormous distances" (III, 911). The persons we dream of lose their total character and are treated as partial objects, either because a part of them is isolated by our dream or because they function altogether as such objects. Now this was precisely what the worldly raw material offered us: the possibility of isolating, as in a frivolous dream, a movement of the shoulders in one person and a movement of the neck in another, not in order to totalize them, but to partition them one from another (III, 900). This is all the more true in the case of the raw material of love, in which each of the beloved beings functions as a partial object, "fragmentary reflection" of a divinity whose partitioned sexes we perceive beneath the total person. In short, the notion of a general law in Proust is inseparable from the production of partial objects and from the production of group truths or of corresponding serial truths.

The second type of machine produces resonances, effects of resonance. The most famous are those of involuntary memory, which affect two moments, a present moment and an earlier one. But desire too has effects of resonance (thus the steeples of Martinville are not a case of reminiscence). Further, art produces resonances that are not those of memory: "Obscure impressions had sometimes... teased my mind like those reminiscences, but these impressions concealed not a past sensation but a new truth, a precious image I was trying to discover by efforts of the same kind as those we make to remember something" (III, 878). This is because art sets up a resonance between two remote objects "by the indescribable link of an alliance of words" (III, 889). We are not to suppose that this new order of production posits the preceding production of partial objects and is established on their basis; this would be to falsify the relation between the two orders, which is not one of foundation. Rather, the relation is like that between a strong and a weak beat, or else, from the viewpoint of the product, between truths of time regained and those of lost time. The order of resonance is distinguished by the faculties of extraction or interpretation it mobilizes and by the quality of its product that is also a mode of production: no longer a general law, of group or series, but a singular essence, a local or localizing essence in the case of the signs of reminiscence, an individuating essence in the case of the signs of art. Resonance does not rest on fragments afforded it by the partial objects; it does not totalize fragments that come to it from elsewhere. It extracts its own fragments itself and sets up a resonance among them according to their own finality, but does not totalize them, because there is always a "hand-to-hand combat," a "struggle" (III, 260, 874). And what is produced by the process of resonance, in the resonance machine, is the singular essence, the Viewpoint superior to the two moments that set up the resonance, breaking with the associative chain that links them: Combray in its essence, as it was never experienced; Combray as Viewpoint, as it was never viewed.

We observed previously that lost time and time regained had the same structure of fragmentation or division. It is not these elements that distinguish them. It would be as false to present lost time as unproductive within its order as to present time regained as totalizing within its order. There are here, on the contrary, two complementary processes of production, each defined by the fragments it creates, its system and its products, the strong beat or the weak beat that occupies it. This is indeed why Proust sees no opposition between the two but defines the production of partial objects as supporting and reinforcing that of resonances. Thus the "vocation" of the man of letters consists not only of the apprenticeship or the undetermined finality (the weak beat), but of the ecstasy or the final goal (strong beat).[7]

What is new in Proust, what constitutes the eternal success and the eternal signification of the madeleine, is not the simple existence of these ecstasies or of these privileged moments, of which literature affords countless examples.[8] Nor is it merely the original way in which Proust presents them and analyzes them in his own style. It is rather the fact that he produces them and that these moments become the effect of a literary machine. Whence the multiplication of resonances at the end of the Search, at Mme de Guermantes's, as if the machine were discovering its maximum efficiency. What is involved is no longer an extraliterary experience that the man of letters reports or profits by, but an artistic experimentation produced by literature, a literary effect, in the sense in which we speak of an electric effect, or an electromagnetic effect. This is the supreme instance in which one can say: the machine works. That art is a machine for producing, and notably for producing certain effects, Proust is most intensely aware — effects on other people, because the readers or spectators will begin to discover, in themselves and outside of themselves, effects analogous to those that the work of art has been able to produce. "Women walk by in the street, different from women of the past, because they are Renoirs, those Renoirs in which we once refused to see women at all. The carriages too are Renoirs, and the water, and the sky" (II, 327). It is in this sense that Proust states that his own books are an optical instrument. And it would be a mistake to find it stupid to have experienced, after reading Proust, phenomena analogous to the resonances he describes. It would be pedantry to wonder if these are cases of paramnesia, of ecmnesia, or of hypermnesia because Proust's originality is to have carved out of this classical realm a figure and a mechanism that did not exist before him. But it is not a matter merely of effects produced upon other people. *It is the work of art that produces within itself and upon itself its own effects, and is filled with them and nourished by them*: the work of art is nourished by the truths it engenders.

Let there be no misunderstanding: what is produced is not simply the interpretation Proust gives of these phenomena of resonance ("the search for causes"). It is, rather, the entire phenomenon itself that is interpretation. Of course, there is an objective aspect of the phenomenon, for example, the flavor of the madeleine as the quality common to two moments. There is also a subjective aspect: the associative chain that links to this flavor all of Combray as it was actually experienced. But if the resonance has both objective and subjective conditions, what it produces is of an altogether different nature: the Essence, the spiritual Equivalent, the Combray that was never seen and that breaks with the subjective chain. This is why producing is different from discovering and creating and why the entire Search turns successively from the observation of things and from the subjective imagination. Now the more the Search insists on this double renunciation, this double purification, the more the narrator realizes that not only does the resonance produce an aesthetic effect, but that the resonance itself can be produced and be in itself an artistic effect.

And no doubt this is what the narrator did not know at the beginning. But the whole Search implies a certain argument between art and life, a question of their relations that will receive an answer only at the book's end (and which will receive its answer precisely in the discovery that art is not only a matter of discovery or creation, but of production). In the course of the Search, if the resonance-as-ecstasy appears as the ultimate goal of life, it is difficult to see what art can add to it, and the narrator suffers the greatest doubts about art. Then later on the resonance appears as the producer of a certain effect, but under given natural conditions, objective and subjective, and by means of the unconscious machine of involuntary memory. But at the end, we see what art is capable of adding to nature: it produces resonances themselves, because *style* sets up a resonance between any two objects and from them extracts a "precious image," *substituting for the determined conditions of an unconscious natural product the free conditions of an artistic production* (III, 878, 889). Henceforth art appears for what it is, the ultimate goal of life, which life cannot realize by itself; and involuntary memory, utilizing only given resonances, is no more than a beginning of art in life, a first stage.[9] Nature or life, still too heavy, have found in art their spiritual equivalent. Even involuntary memory has found its spiritual equivalent, pure thought, both produced and producing.

The entire interest thus shifts from the privileged natural moments to the artistic machine capable of producing or reproducing them, of multiplying them: the Book. In this regard, we can scarcely avoid the comparison with Joyce and his machine for producing *epiphanies*. For Joyce too begins by seeking the secret of epiphanies within the object, first within significant contents or ideal significations, then in the subjective experience of an aesthete. It

is only when the significant contents and the ideal significations have collapsed and given way to a multiplicity
of fragments, to chaos — but in addition, the subjective
forms to a chaotic and multiple impersonal reality — that
the work of art assumes its full meaning, that is, exactly
all the meanings one wants it to have according to its functioning; the essential point being that it functions, that
the machine works. Then the artist, and the reader in his
wake, is the one who "disentangles" and "re-embodies":
setting up a resonance between two objects, he produces
the epiphany, releasing the precious image from the natural conditions that determine it, in order to reincarnate
it in the chosen artistic conditions.[10] "Signifier and signified fuse by means of a short-circuit poetically necessary
but ontologically gratuitous and unforeseen. The coded
language does not refer to an objective cosmos, external
to the work; its comprehension is valid only within the
work and is conditioned by the latter's structure. The
work as a Whole proposes new linguistic conventions to
which it is subject and itself becomes the key to its own
code."[11] Further, the work is a whole, in a new sense, only
by virtue of these new linguistic conventions.

There remains the third Proustian order, that of universal alteration and death. Mme de Guermantes's salon,
with the aging of its guests, makes us see the distortion
of features, the fragmentation of gestures, the loss of co-
ordination of muscles, the changes in color, the formation of moss, lichen, patches of mold on bodies, sublime
disguises, sublime senilities. Everywhere the approach of
death, the sentiment of the presence of a "terrible thing,"
the impression of an ending or even of a final catastrophe

upon a déclassé world that is not only governed by forgetting but corroded by time ("slackened or broken, the machinery's parts no longer functioned..." [III, 957].)

Now, this final order raises all the more problems in that it seems to fit into the other two. Beneath the ecstasies, was there not already lurking the idea of death and the slipping away of the earlier moment? Thus when the narrator leaned down to unbutton his boot, everything began exactly as in ecstasy, the present moment set up a resonance with the earlier one, resuscitating the grandmother leaning down; but joy had given way to an intolerable anguish, the pairing of the two moments had broken down, yielding to a sudden disappearance of the earlier one, in a certainty of death and nothingness (II, 758). In the same way, the succession of distinct selves in love affairs, or even in the same love, already contained a long train of suicides and deaths (III, 1037). However, whereas the first two orders raised no special problem of reconciliation (though the one represented a weak beat, lost time, and the other a strong beat, time regained), there is now, on the contrary, a reconciliation to be found, a contradiction to be surmounted, between this third order and the other two (which is why Proust speaks here of "the gravest objections" to his enterprise). This is because the partial objects and selves of the first order deal out death to each other, each remaining indifferent to the other's death; they do not yet afford, then, *the idea of death* as uniformly imbuing all fragments, carrying them toward a universal end. With all the more reason, a "contradiction" is manifest between the survival of the second order and the nothingness of the third, between "the fixity of memory" and "the alteration of beings," between the final ecstatic goal and the catastrophic ending (II, 759–60; III, 988). This contradiction is not resolved in the recollection of the grandmother and therefore requires further exploration: "I certainly did not know if I would one day extract some bit of truth from this painful and at the moment incomprehensible impression, but I knew that if I ever did, it could only come from that individual, spontaneous impression that had been neither traced by my intelligence nor attenuated by my cowardice, but which death itself, the sudden revelation of death, had imprinted upon me as though by a bolt of lightning, according to a supernatural and inhuman emblem, a double and mysterious furrow" (II, 759). The contradiction appears here in its most acute form: the first two orders were productive, and it is for this reason that their reconciliation raised no special problem; but the third order, dominated by the idea of death, seems absolutely catastrophic and unproductive. Can we conceive a machine capable of extracting something from this kind of painful impression and of producing certain truths? So long as we cannot, the work of art encounters "the gravest objections."

Of what, then, does this idea of death consist, which is so different from the aggression of the first order (somewhat as, in psychoanalysis, the death instinct is distinguished from partial destructive impulses)? It consists of a certain effect of Time. With two given states of the same person — the earlier that we remember, the present that we experience — the impression of aging from one to the other has the effect of pushing the earlier moment "into a past more than remote, almost improbable," as if geological periods had intervened (III, 939–40). For "in the appraisal of time gone by, it is the first step alone that is difficult. At first we feel great pain at realizing that so much time has passed and then that more has not passed. We had never dreamed that the eighteenth century was so far away, and afterwards we can scarcely believe that there can still remain some churches from the thirteenth century" (III, 933). It is in this fashion that the movement of time, from past to present, is doubled by a *forced movement of greater amplitude*, in the contrary direction, which sweeps away the two moments, emphasizes the gap between them, and pushes the past still farther back into time. It is this second movement that constitutes, in time, a "horizon." We must not confuse it with the echo of resonance; it dilates time infinitely, while resonance contracts time to the maximum degree. The idea of death is henceforth less a severance than an effect of mixture or confusion because the amplitude of the forced movement is as much taken up by the living as by the dead; all are dying, half dead, or racing to the grave (III, 977). But this half-death is also of giant stature because, at the heart of the excessive amplitude of the movement, we can describe men as monstrous beings, "occupying within Time a much more considerable place than the limited one that is reserved for them in space, a place on the contrary extended measurelessly because they touch simultaneously, like giants, plunged into the years, periods so remote from each other — between which so many days have taken their place — within time" (III, 1048). Thus, in the same way, we are prepared to surmount the objection or the contradiction. The idea of death ceases to be an "objection" provided we can attach it to an order of production, thus giving it its place in the work of art. The forced movement of great amplitude is a machine that produces the effect of withdrawal or the idea of death. And in this effect, it is time itself that becomes sensuous: "Time that is usually not visible, that in order to become so seeks bodies and, wherever it finds them, seizes upon them in order to project its magic lantern upon them," quartering the fragments and features of an aging face, according to its "inconceivable dimension" (III, 924–25). A machine of the third order comes to join the preceding two, a machine that produces the forced movement and thereby the idea of death.

What has happened in the recollection of the grandmother? A forced movement has meshed gears with a resonance. The amplitude bearing the idea of death has swept away the resonant moments as such. But the violent contradiction between time regained and lost time is resolved provided we attach each of the two to its order of production. The entire Search sets three kinds of machines to work in the production of the Book: *machines of partial objects (impulses), machines of resonance (Eros), machines of forced movement (Thanatos)*. Each one produces truths, because it is the nature of truth to be produced and to be produced as an effect of time: lost time, by fragmentation of partial objects; time regained, by resonance; lost time that has been lost in another way, by amplitude of the forced movement, this loss having then passed into the work and become the condition of its form.

CHAPTER 12

Style

But just what is this form, and how are the orders of production or of truth, the machines, organized within each other? None has a function of totalization. The essential point is that the parts of the Search remain partitioned, fragmented, *without anything lacking*: eternally partial parts, open boxes and sealed vessels, swept on by time without forming a whole or presupposing one, without lacking anything in this quartering, and denouncing in advance every organic unity we might seek to introduce into it. When Proust compares his work to a cathedral or to a gown, it is not to identify himself with a Logos as a splendid totality but, on the contrary, to emphasize his right to incompletion, to seams and patches (III, 1033–34). Time is not a whole, for the simple reason that it is itself the instance that prevents the whole. The world has no significant contents according to which we could systematize it nor ideal significations according to which we could regulate and hierarchize it. Nor has the subject an associative chain that could surround the world or stand for its unity. To turn toward the subject is no more fruitful than to observe the object: "interpreting" dissolves the one no less than the other. Further, any associative chain is broken and gives way to a Viewpoint superior to the subject. But these viewpoints upon the world, veritable Essences, do not in turn form a unity or a totality; one might say rather that a universe corresponds to each, not communicating with the others, affirming an irreducible difference as profound as that of the astronomic worlds. Even in art, where the viewpoints are the purest, "each artist seems then like the citizen of an unknown country, a fatherland he himself has forgotten, different from the one from which will come, heading for the Earth, another great artist."[1] And this seems a good definition of the status of essence: an individuating viewpoint superior to the individuals themselves, breaking with their chains of associations; essence appears *alongside* these chains, incarnated in a closed fragment, *adjacent* to what it overwhelms, *contiguous* to what it reveals. Even the Church, a viewpoint superior to the landscape, has the effect of partitioning this landscape and rises up itself, at the turn of the road, like the ultimate partitioned fragment adjacent to the series that is defined by it. That is, the Essences, like the Laws, have no power to unify or to totalize. "A river passing under the bridges of a city was shown from a *viewpoint* that made it seem quite dislocated, spread out in one place like a lake, narrowed in another to a thread, broken elsewhere by the interposition of a hill crowned with woods where the city dweller goes evenings to enjoy the cool of the evening; and the very rhythm of this discomposed city was effected only by the inflexible vertical of the steeples that did not so much raise as, according to the plumb line of weight, marking the cadence as in a triumphal procession, seemed to suspend beneath themselves the whole more confused mass of houses tiered in the mist, along the banks of the disconnected and crumpled river" (I, 839–40).

The problem is raised by Proust on several levels: What constitutes the unity of a work? What makes us "communicate" with a work? What constitutes the unity of art, if there is such a thing? We have given up seeking a unity that would unify the parts, a whole that would totalize the fragments. For it is the character and nature of the parts or fragments to exclude the Logos both as logical unity and as organic totality. But there is, there must be a unity that is the unity *of* this very multiplicity, a whole that is the whole *of* just these fragments: a One and a Whole that would not be the principle but, on the contrary, "the effect" of the multiplicity and of its disconnected parts. One and Whole that would function as effect, effect of machines, instead of as principles. A communication that would not be posited in principle but would result from the operation of the machines and their detached parts, their noncommunicating fragments. Philosophically, Leibniz was the first to raise the problem of a communication resulting from sealed parts or from what does not communicate. How are we to conceive the communication of the "monads" that have neither door nor window? Leibniz answers meretriciously that the closed "monads" all possess the same stock, enveloping and expressing the same world in the infinite series of their predicates, each content to have a region of expression distinct from that of the others, all thus being different viewpoints toward the same world that God causes them to envelop. Leibniz's answer thus restores a preceding totality in the form of a God who slips the same stock of world or of information ("preestablished harmony") into each monad and who sets up among their solitudes a spontaneous "correspondence." This can no longer be the case for Proust, for whom so many various worlds correspond to viewpoints toward the world and for whom unity, totality, and communication can result only from machines and not constitute a preestablished stock.[2]

Once again, the problem of the work of art is the problem of a unity and a totality that would be neither logical nor organic, that is, neither presupposed by the parts as a lost unity or a fragmented totality nor formed or prefigured by them in the course of a logical development or of an organic evolution. Proust is all the more conscious of this problem in that he assigns it an origin: Balzac was able to raise the problem and thereby brought into existence a new type of work of art. For it is the same mistake, the same incomprehension of Balzac's genius, that makes us suppose he had a vague logical idea of the unity of the *Human Comedy* beforehand or even that this unity is organically constituted as the work advances. Actually, the unity results and is discovered by Balzac as an *effect* of his books. An "effect" is not an illusion: "He realized suddenly, by projecting upon them a retrospective illumination, that they would be more beautiful united in a cycle in which the same characters would return and added to his work, in this connection, a brushstroke, the last and most sublime. A subsequent unity, not a factitious one ... not fictive, perhaps even more real for being subsequent..." (III, 161). The mistake would be to suppose that the consciousness or the discovery of unity, coming afterwards, does not change the nature and the function of this One itself. Balzac's One or Whole is so special that

it results from the parts without altering the fragmentation or disparity of those parts, and, like the dragons of
Balbec or Vinteuil's phrase, is itself valid as a part alongside others, adjacent to others: unity "appears (but relat-
ing now to the whole) like any one fragment composed
separately," like a last localized brushstroke, not like a
general varnishing. So that, in a certain sense, Balzac *has
no style*: not that he says "everything," as Sainte-Beuve supposes, but the fragments of silence and of speech, what
he says and what he does not say, are distributed in a fragmentation that the whole ultimately confirms because it
results from it, rather than corrects or transcends. "In Balzac there coexist, *not digested, not yet transformed,* all the
elements of a style-to-come that does not exist. Style does
not suggest, does not reflect: it explains, *explicates.* It explicates moreover by means of the most striking images,
but *not dissolved into the rest,* which make us understand
what he means the way we make it understood in conversation if we have an inspired conversation, but *without being concerned with harmony and without intervening.*"[3]

Can we say that Proust, too, has no style? Is it possible to say that Proust's sentence, inimitable or too readily
imitable, in any case immediately recognizable, endowed
with a syntax and a vocabulary that are extremely idio-
syncratic, producing effects that must be designated by
Proust's own name, is nonetheless without style? And how
does the absence of style become here the inspired power
of a new literature? We should have to compare the whole
finale of *Time Regained* with Balzac's *Foreword*: the system
of plants has replaced what the Animal was for Balzac;
the worlds have replaced the milieu; essences have re-

placed characteristics; silent interpretation has replaced "inspired conversation." But what is retained, and raised to a new value, is the "terrifying confusion," especially without concern for the whole or for harmony. Style here does not propose to describe nor to suggest: as in Balzac, it is explicative, it explicates with images. It is nonstyle because it is identified with "interpreting," pure and without subject, and multiplies the viewpoints toward the sentence, within the sentence. The sentence is thus like the river that appears "quite dislocated, spread out in one place like a lake, narrowed in another to a thread, broken elsewhere by the interposition of a hill." Style is the explication of the signs, at different rates of development, following the associative chains proper to each of them, gaining in each case the breaking point of essence as Viewpoint: whence the role of the incidental, the subordinate, of comparisons that express in an image this process of explication, the image being a good one if it explicates well, always clashing, never sacrificing to the so-called beauty of the whole. Or rather, style begins with two *different* objects, distant even if they are contiguous: it may be that these two objects resemble each other objectively, are of the same kind; it may be that they are linked subjectively by a chain of association. Style will have to sweep all this on, like a river bearing the substances of its bed; but that is not what is essential. What is essential occurs when the sentence achieves a Viewpoint proper to each of the two objects, but precisely a viewpoint that we must call proper to the object because the object is already dislocated by it, as if the viewpoint were divided into a thousand various noncommunicating viewpoints, so that, the same operation being performed for the other object, the view-points can be set within each other, setting up resonance among themselves, a little as the land and the sea exchange their viewpoint in Elstir's paintings. This is the "effect" of explicative style: in relation to two given objects, *it produces partial objects* (it produces *them* as partial objects set one within another), *it produces effects of resonance and forced movements.* Such is the image as produced by style. This production in the pure state is what we find in art, painting, literature, or music, above all music. And as we descend the degrees of essence, from the signs of art to the signs of Nature, love, or even worldliness, there is necessarily reintroduced a minimum of objective description and associative suggestion; but this is only because essence here has material conditions of incarnation that are then substituted for the free artistic spiritual conditions, as Joyce would say.[4] But style is never a matter of the man, it is always a matter of essence (nonstyle). It is never a matter of viewpoint but is constituted by the coexistence in the same sentence of an infinite series of viewpoints according to which the object is dislocated, sets up a resonance, or is amplified.

Hence it is not style that guarantees unity—because style must receive its unity from elsewhere. Nor is it essence, because essence as viewpoint is perpetually fragmenting and fragmented. What then is this very special mode of unity irreducible to any "unification," this very special unity that appears afterwards, that assures the exchange of viewpoints as it does the communication of essences, and that appears according to the law of essence, itself a fragment alongside others, a final brushstroke or a localized part?

The answer is as follows: in a world reduced to a multi-plicity of chaos, it is only the formal structure of the work of art, insofar as it does not refer to anything else, that can serve as unity—afterwards (or as Umberto Eco says, "the work as a whole proposes new linguistic conventions to which it submits, and itself becomes the key to its own code"). But the whole problem is to know on what this formal structure rests and how it gives the parts and the style a unity that they would not have without it. Now, we have previously seen, in the most diverse directions, the importance of a *transversal dimension* in Proust's work: transversality.[5] It is transversality that permits us, in the train, not to unify the viewpoints of a landscape, but to bring them into communication according to the land-scape's own dimension, in its own dimension, whereas they remain noncommunicating according to their own di-mension. It is transversality that constitutes the singular unity and totality of the Méséglise Way and of the Guer-mantes Way, without suppressing their difference or dis-tance: "between these routes certain transversals were es-tablished" (III, 1029). It is transversality that establishes the profanations and is obsessed by the bumblebee, the transversal insect that causes the partitioned sexes to com-municate. It is transversality that assures the transmission of a ray, from one universe to another as different as as-tronomical worlds. The new linguistic convention, the for-mal structure of the work, is therefore transversality, which passes through the entire sentence, which proceeds from one sentence to another in the entire book, and which even unites Proust's book to those he preferred, by Nerval, Chateaubriand, Balzac. For if a work of art communicates

with a public and even gives rise to that public, if it communicates with the other works of the same artist and
gives rise to them, if it communicates with other works
of other artists and gives rise to works to come, it is always within this dimension of transversality, in which unity
and totality are established for themselves, without unifying or totalizing objects or subjects.[6] This additional
dimension is added to those that are occupied by characters, events, and parts of the Search—it is a dimension
in time without common measure with the dimensions
they occupy in space. This dimension causes the viewpoints to interpenetrate and brings into the communication the sealed vessels that nonetheless remain closed:
Odette with Swann, the mother with the narrator, Albertine with the narrator, and then, as a last "brushstroke,"
the old Odette with the Duc de Guermantes—each one
is a captive, and yet all communicate transversally (III,
1029). Such is time, the dimension of the narrator, which
has the power to be the whole *of* these parts without totalizing them, the unity *of* these parts without unifying
them.

Presence and Function of Madness: The Spider

The problem of art and madness in Proust's work has not been raised. Perhaps this question has little or no meaning. Still less: was Proust mad? This question certainly has no meaning. Our concern is only with the presence of madness in Proust's work and with the distribution, use, or function of this presence.

For madness at least appears and functions under a different modality in two main characters, Charlus and Albertine. From Charlus's first appearances, his strange gaze and his eyes themselves are characterized as those of a spy, a thief, a salesman, a detective, or a *madman* (I, 751). Ultimately Morel experiences a well-founded terror at the notion that Charlus is animated by a sort of criminal madness against him (III, 804–6). And throughout, people sense in Charlus the presence of a madness that makes him infinitely more terrifying than if he were merely immoral or perverse, sinful or blameworthy. Perversity "alarms because of the madness sensed within it, much more than because of any immorality. Mme de Surgis had not the slightest sense of a conscious moral sentiment, and with regard to her sons she would have accepted anything that mere worldly interest, comprehensible to anyone, might have discounted and explained. But she forbade them to continue seeing M. de Charlus when she learned that, by a sort of clockwork mechanism, he was somehow fatally impelled, on each visit, to pinch their chins and to make them pinch each others'. She experienced that anxious feeling of physical mystery that makes one wonder if the neighbor with whom one had such good relations may not suffer from cannibalism, and to the Baron's repeated question: won't I be seeing the young men soon? she replied, conscious of the thunderbolts she was drawing down upon her head, that they were very much involved with their studies, preparations for a journey, etc. Irresponsibility aggravates sins and even crimes, whatever we say. If Landru, supposing he actually killed his wives, did so for (resistible) reasons of worldly interest, he might be pardoned, but not if he murdered out of motives of some irresistible sadism" (III, 205). Beyond responsibility for sins, madness is innocence of crime.

That Charlus is mad is a probability from the beginning, a quasi-certainty at the end. In Albertine's case, madness is rather a posthumous likelihood that retrospectively casts over her words and gestures, over her entire life, a new and disturbing light in which Morel too is involved. "In actuality," Andrée says, "Albertine felt it was a kind of criminal madness, and I've often wondered if it wasn't after a thing like that, having led to a suicide in a family, that she killed herself" (III). What is this mixture of madness-crime-irresponsibility-sexuality, which doubtless has something to do with Proust's cherished theme of parricide, but which nonetheless does not come down to the all-too-familiar Oedipal schema? A sort of innocence in crimes of madness, intolerable as such, including suicide?

Take first of all the case of Charlus. Charlus immediately presents himself as a strong personality, an imperial individuality. But in fact this individuality is an empire, a galaxy that conceals or contains many unknown things: what is Charlus's secret? The entire galaxy is structured around two notable points: the eyes, the voice. The eyes sometimes flashing with overbearing brilliance, sometimes shifting with inquisitive intensity, sometimes feverishly active, sometimes dim with indifference. The voice, which makes the virile content of what is spoken coexist with an effeminate manner of expression. Charlus presents himself as an enormous flashing indicator, a huge optical and vocal vessel: anyone who listens to Charlus or who meets his gaze finds himself confronting a secret, a mystery to be penetrated, to be interpreted, which he presents from the start as likely to proceed to the point of madness. And the necessity of interpreting Charlus is based on the fact that this Charlus himself interprets, unceasingly interprets, as if that were his own madness, as if that were already his delirium, a delirium of interpretation.

From the Charlus-galaxy proceeds a series of utterances punctuated by the vacillating gaze. *Three major speeches* to the narrator, which find their occasion in the signs Charlus interprets, as prophet and soothsayer, but which also find their destination in signs Charlus proposes to the narrator, here reduced to the role of disciple or pupil. Yet the essential of these speeches is elsewhere, in the words deliberately organized, in the phrases sovereignly arranged, in a Logos that calculates and transcends the signs of which it makes use: Charlus, master of the logos. And from this point of view, the three major speeches have a common structure, despite their differences of rhythm and intensity. A first phase of denial, in which

Charlus says to the narrator: you interest me, don't suppose that you interest me, but.... A second phase of distancing, in which Charlus says: between you and me, the distance is infinite, but just for that reason we can complement each other, I am offering you a contract.... And a third, unexpected phase, in which it seems that suddenly the logos goes haywire, traversed by something that can no longer be organized. It is charged with a power of another order, rage, insult, provocation, profanation, sadistic fantasy, demential gesture, the eruption of madness. This is already true of the first speech, filled with a noble tenderness but finding its aberrant conclusion the next day on the beach, in M. de Charlus's coarse and prophetic remark: "You don't give a damn about your old grandmother, do you, you little snot...." The second speech is interrupted by a fantasy of Charlus imagining a comical scene in which Bloch engages in fisticuffs with his father and pummels his mother's decaying carcass: "As he spoke these dreadful and almost lunatic words, M. de Charlus squeezed my arm until it hurt." Finally, the third speech is blurted out in the violent ordeal of the trampled hat. It is true that it is not Charlus this time, but the narrator who tramples the hat; yet we shall see that the narrator possesses a madness valid for all the others, communicating with Charlus's as with Albertine's, and capable of replacing them in order to anticipate or develop their effects.[1]

If Charlus is the apparent master of the Logos, his speeches are nonetheless disturbed by involuntary signs that resist the sovereign organization of language and cannot be mastered in words and phrases, but rout the logos and involve us in another realm. "From several splendid utterances that tinged his hatreds, one felt that even if there was an occasion of offended pride or disappointed love, even if there was no more than a certain rancor, some sort of sadism, a teasing disposition, an idée fixe, this man was capable of murder. . . ." Signs of violence and madness constituting a certain pathos, counter to and beneath the deliberate signs arranged by "logic and fine language." It is this pathos that will now reveal itself as such, in Charlus's appearances where he speaks less and less from the summit of his sovereign organization and increasingly betrays himself in the course of a long social and physical decomposition. This is no longer the world of speeches and of their vertical communications expressing a hierarchy of rules and positions, but the world of anarchic encounters, of violent accidents, with their aberrant transverse communications. This is the Charlus-Jupien encounter, in which is revealed the long-awaited secret: the homosexuality of Charlus. But is this really Charlus's secret? For what is discovered is less homosexuality, long since foreseeable and suspected, than a general system that makes such homosexuality into a particular case of a deeper universal madness inextricably intermingling innocence and crime. What is discovered is the world in which one no longer speaks, the silent vegetal universe, the madness of the Flowers whose fragmented theme punctuates the encounter with Jupien.

The logos is a huge Animal whose parts unite in a whole and are unified under a principle or a leading idea; but the pathos is a vegetal realm consisting of cellular elements that communicate only indirectly, only marginally, so that no totalization, no unification, can unite this world of ultimate fragments. It is a schizoid universe of closed vessels, of cellular regions, where contiguity itself is a distance: the world of sex. This is what Charlus himself teaches us beyond his speeches. As individuals possessing both sexes, though "separated by a partition," we must cause the intervention of a galactic structure of eight elements, in which the male part or the female part of a man or woman can enter into relation with the female part or the male part of another woman or man *(ten combinations for the eight elements: an elementary combination will be defined by the encounter of one individual's male or female part with the male or female part of another individual. This produces: male part of a man and female part of a woman, but also male part of a woman and female part of a man, male part of a man and female part of another man, male part of a man and male part of another man ... etc.)* Aberrant relations between closed vessels; the bumblebee that constitutes the communication between flowers and loses its proper animal value becomes in relation to the latter merely a marginalized fragment, a disparate element in an apparatus of vegetal reproduction.

This may be a composition recognizable everywhere in the Search: starting from a first galaxy that constitutes an apparently circumscribed set, unifiable and totalizable, one or more series are produced, and these series emerge in their turn as a new galaxy, this time decentered or eccentric, consisting of circling closed cells, disparate shifting fragments that follow the transverse vanishing traces. Take the case of Charlus: the first galaxy features his eyes, his voice; then the series of speeches; then the ultimate disturbing world of signs and cells, of closed and communicating vessels that compose Charlus and can be opened or interpreted according to the vanishing trace of an aging star and its satellites ("M. de Charlus navigating by means of his whole enormous body, involuntarily dragging behind him one of those hooligans or beggars that his mere passage now infallibly produced from even the most apparently deserted nooks and crannies..." [III, 204]). Yet the same composition governs Albertine's story: the galaxy of girls from which Albertine slowly extracts herself; the major series of her two successive jealousies; finally the coexistence of all the cells in which Albertine imprisons herself in her lies, but also is imprisoned by the narrator, a new galaxy that recomposes the first in its own fashion, because the end of love is like a return to the initial indivisibility of the *jeunes filles*. And Albertine's vanishing trace compared to that of Charlus. Further, in the exemplary passage of kissing Albertine, the vigilant narrator starts with Albertine's face, a mobile set in which the beauty spot stands out as a singular feature, then as the narrator's lips approach Albertine's cheek, the desired face passes through a series of successive planes to which correspond so many Albertines, beauty spot leaping from one to the next; ending with the final blur in which Albertine's face is released and undone, and in which the narrator, losing the use of her lips, her eyes, her nose, recognizes "from these hateful signs" that he is in the process of kissing the beloved being.

If this great law of composition and decomposition is as valid for Albertine as for Charlus, it is because it is the law of loves and of sexuality. Intersexual loves, notably the narrator's for Albertine, are in no way a mask for

Proust's own homosexuality. On the contrary, these loves form the initial set, from which will be derived the two homosexual series represented by Albertine and by Charlus ("the two sexes will die each apart from the other"). But these series open in their turn into a transexual universe where the partitioned, sealed sexes regroup within each one in order to communicate with those of the other along aberrant transverse lines. Now if it is true that a sort of surface normality characterizes the first level or the first set, the series that proceed from it on the second level are marked by all the sufferings, anguishes, and culpabilities of what is called neurosis: the curse of Oedipus and the prophecy of Samson. But the third level restores a vegetal innocence within decomposition, assigning to madness its absolving function in a world where the vessels explode or close up again, crimes and sequestrations that constitute "the human comedy" in Proust's manner, through which develops a new and final power that overwhelms all the others, a mad power indeed, that of the Search itself insofar as it unites the policeman and the madman, the spy and the salesman, the interpreter and the claimant.

If Albertine's story and that of Charlus obey the same general law, madness has nonetheless a very different form and function in each case, and is not distributed in the same way. We see three main differences between the Charlus-madness and the Albertine-madness. The first is that Charlus possesses a superior individuation as an imperial individuality. Charlus' problem henceforth concerns communication. The questions "what is Charlus hiding?" and "what are the secret cells his individuality conceals?"

refer to communications that must be discovered, to their aberrancy, so that the Charlus-madness can be manifested, interpreted, and can interpret itself, only by means of violent accidental encounters, in relation to the new milieus in which Charlus is plunged that will act as so many developers, inductors, communicators (encounters with the narrator, encounter with Jupien, encounter with the Verdurins, encounter at the brothel). Albertine's case is different, because her problem concerns individuation itself: which of the girls is she? How to extract and select her from the undifferentiated group of *jeunes filles*? Here, it seems that her communications are initially given, but what is specifically hidden is the mystery of her individuation, and this mystery can be fathomed only insofar as the communications are interrupted, forcefully brought to a halt, Albertine made a captive, immured, sequestered. A second difference proceeds from this one. Charlus is the master of discourse, with him everything happens by means of words, but on the other hand nothing happens in words. Charlus's investments are above all verbal, so that things or objects present themselves as involuntary signs turned against discourse, sometimes making speech go haywire, sometimes forming a counterlanguage that develops in the silence of encounters. Albertine's relation to language, on the contrary, consists of humble lies and not of royal deviance. This is because, in her, investment remains an investment in the thing or the object that will be expressed in language itself, provided it fragments language's deliberate signs and subjects them to the laws of lying that here insert the involuntary: then everything can happen in language (including silence) precisely because nothing happens by means of language.

There is a third great difference. At the end of the nineteenth century and at the beginning of the twentieth, psychiatry established a very interesting distinction between two kinds of sign-deliriums: deliriums of a paranoiac type of interpretation and deliriums of an erotomaniacal or jealous type of demand. The former have an insidious beginning, a gradual development that depends essentially on endogenous forces, spreading in a general network that mobilizes the series of verbal investments. The latter begin much more abruptly and are linked to real or imagined external occasions; they depend on a sort of "postulate" concerning a specific object, and enter into limited constellations; they are not so much a delirium of ideas passing through an extended system of verbal investments as a delirium of action animated by an intensive investment in the object (erotomania, for instance, presents itself as a delirious pursuit of the beloved, rather than as a delirious illusion of being loved). *These second deliriums form a succession of finite linear processes, while the first form radiating circular sets.* We are not saying, of course, that Proust applies to his characters a psychiatric distinction that was being elaborated in his era. But Charlus and Albertine, respectively, trace paths within the Search that correspond to this distinction, in a very specific fashion. We have tried to show this for Charlus, an extreme paranoiac: his first appearances are insidious, the development and precipitation of his delirium testifies to redoubtable endogenous forces, and all his verbal interpretative madness masks the more mysterious signs of the nonlanguage working within him; in short, the enormous Charlus network. But on the other hand, Albertine: herself an object, or in pursuit of objects on her own account; launching postulates with which she is familiar, or else imprisoned by the narrator in a dead-end postulate of which she is the victim (*Albertine necessarily and a priori guilty, to love without being loved, to be harsh, cruel, and deceptive with what one loves*). Erotomaniac and jealous, though it is also and above all the narrator who shows himself to be these things with her. And the series of the two jealousies with regard to Albertine, inseparable in each case from the external occasion, constituting successive processes. And the signs of language and of nonlanguage insert themselves here one within the other, forming the limited constellations of lying. A whole delirium of action and of demand, quite different from Charlus's delirium of ideas and interpretation.

But why must we confuse in one and the same case Albertine and the narrator's behavior with regard to Albertine? Everything tells us, it is true, that the narrator's jealousy concerns an Albertine profoundly jealous with regard to her own "objects." And the narrator's erotomania with regard to Albertine (the delirious pursuit of the beloved with no illusion of being loved) is interrupted by Albertine's own erotomania, long suspected, then confirmed as the secret that provoked the narrator's jealousy. And the narrator's demand, to imprison and immure Albertine, masks Albertine's demands realized too late. It is also true that Charlus's case is analogous: there is no way of distinguishing the labor of Charlus's interpretative delirium from the narrator's long labor of interpretative delirium concerning Charlus. But we ask exactly whence comes the necessity of these partial identifications and what is their function in the Search?

Jealous of Albertine, interpreter of Charlus — what is the narrator, ultimately, in himself? To accept the necessity of distinguishing the narrator and the hero as two subjects (subject of *énonciation* and subject of *énoncé*) would be to refer the Search to a system of subjectivity (a doubled, split subject) that is alien to it. There is less a narrator than a machine of the Search, and less a hero than the arrangements by which the machine functions under one or another configuration, according to one or another articulation, for one or another purpose, for one or another production. It is only in this sense that we can ask what the narrator-hero is, who does not function as a subject. The reader at least is struck by the insistence with which Proust presents the narrator as incapable of seeing, of perceiving, of remembering, of understanding . . . , etc. This is the great opposition to the Goncourt or Sainte-Beuve method. A constant theme of the Search, which culminates in the Verdurins' country house ("I see that you like drafts of fresh air. . . . [II, 944]). Actually the narrator has no organs or never has those he needs, those he wants. He notices this himself in the scene of the first kiss he gives Albertine, when he complains that we have no adequate organ to perform such an action that fills our lips, stuffs our nose, and closes our eyes. Indeed the narrator is an enormous Body without organs.

But what is a body without organs? The spider too sees nothing, perceives nothing, remembers nothing. She receives only the slightest vibration at the edge of her web, which propagates itself in her body as an intensive wave and sends her leaping to the necessary place. Without eyes, without nose, without mouth, she answers only to signs, the merest sign surging through her body and causing her to spring upon her prey. The Search is not constructed like a cathedral or like a gown, but like a web. The spider-Narrator, whose web is the Search being spun, being woven by each thread stirred by one sign or another: the web and the spider, the web and the body are one and the same machine. Though endowed with an extreme sensibility and a prodigious memory, the narrator has no organs insofar as he is deprived of any voluntary and organized use of such faculties. On the other hand, a faculty functions within him when constrained and obliged to do so; and the corresponding organ wakens within him, but as an *intensive outline* roused by the waves that provoke its involuntary use. Involuntary sensibility, involuntary memory, involuntary thought that are, each time, like the intense totalizing reactions of the organless body to signs of one nature or another. It is this body, this spider's web, that opens or seals each of the tiny cells that a sticky thread of the Search happens to touch. Strange plasticity of the narrator: it is this spider-body of the narrator, the spy, the policeman, the jealous lover, the interpreter—the madman—the universal schizophrenic who will send out a thread toward Charlus the paranoiac, another thread toward Albertine the erotomaniac, in order to make them so many marionettes of his own delirium, so many intensive powers of his organless body, so many profiles of his own madness.

Notes

3. Apprenticeship

1. II, 66: "Françoise was the first to give me the example (which I was not to understand until later...)."

2. III, 888–96. It must not be supposed that Proust's critique of objectivism can be applied to what is called today the *new novel*. The new novel's methods of describing the object have a meaning only in relation to the subjective modifications that they serve to reveal, and, without them, would remain imperceptible. The new novel remains under the sign of hieroglyphs and implied truths.

5. The Secondary Role of Memory

1. III, 889 ("...or even, as in life...").

8. Antilogos

1. The dialectic is not separable from these extrinsic characteristics; thus Bergson defines it by two characteristics: the conversation between friends and the conventional signification of words (see *La Pensée et le mouvant*, Presses Universitaires de France, pp. 86–88).

2. III, 713. It is in this pastiche of the Goncourts that Proust carries furthest his critique of *observation*, a critique that is one of the constant themes of the Search.

3. II, 756. On the intelligence that must "come after," see III, 880, and the whole preface to *Contre Sainte-Beuve*.

4. II, 260: "Monsieur de Norpois, concerned by the turn events were about to take, knew perfectly well that it was not by the word *Peace*, or by the word *War*, that he would discover their significations, but by another, banal in appearance, terrible or consecrated, which the diplomat, with the help of his code, would immediately be able to read, and to which, in order to

safeguard the dignity of France, he would reply by another word just as banal but under which the minister of the enemy nation would immediately see: War."

5. Cf. Aeschylus, *Agamemnon*, 460–502.

9. Cells and Vessels

1. We have already remarked that the madeleine is a case of successful *explication* (contrary to the three trees, for example, whose content remains lost forever). But only half successful; for, though "the essence" is already invoked, the narrator remains at the point of the associative chain that does not yet explain "why this memory made him so happy." It is only at the end of the Search that the theory and experience of Essence are given their final status.

2. I, 87: "...it was not by the accident of a simple association of thought..."

3. I, 610–11: "It was a long and cruel suicide of that self within me who loved Gilberte that I continually sought to effect, with the clear awareness not only of what I was doing in the present, but of what would result from it for the future."

4. On the two associative movements in opposite directions, see I, 660. It is this disappointment that will be recompensed, without being made good, by the pleasures of genealogy or of the etymology of proper names.

5. As Georges Poulet puts it: "The Proustian universe is a universe in fragments, of which the fragments contain other universes, these too, in their turn, in fragments.... The temporal discontinuity is itself preceded, even governed, by a still more radical discontinuity, that of space." However, Poulet upholds in Proust's work the rights of a continuity and of a unity whose very particular original nature he does not attempt to define; this is because, further, he tends to deny the originality or the specificity of Proustian time. (On the pretext that this time has nothing to do with a Bergsonian duration, he asserts that it is a spatialized time.) The problem of a world in fragments, in its most general purport, has been raised by Maurice Blanchot.

The question is to discover what is the unity or nonunity of a certain world, once it is said that such a world neither supposes nor forms a whole: "If we say fragment we must not only say fragmentation of an already existing reality, nor a moment of a whole still to come.... In the violence of the fragment, an entirely different relation is given to us," "a new relation with the External World," "an affirmation irreducible to unity," which cannot be reduced to aphoristic form.

6. II, 365–66: "I learned, from these detestable signs, that at last I was in the act of kissing Albertine's cheek."

7. For Odette as for Albertine, Proust invokes those fragments of truth that, introduced by the beloved in order to authenticate a lie, have on the contrary the effect of revealing it. But before bearing on the truth or falsity of a narrative, this "disagreement" bears on the words themselves that, united in a single sentence, have very diverse origins and connotations.

8. I, 655: "The train changed direction ... and I was sorry to have lost my strip of pink sky when I caught sight of it again, but red this time, in the opposite window, which it abandoned at a second turning of the roadbed; so that I spent my time running from one window to the other in order to relate, to remount the intermittent and opposite fragments of my splendid and changeable scarlet morning, and to gain a total view of it, a continuous picture." This text certainly invokes a continuity and a totality, but the essential point is to know where these are elaborated—neither in the viewpoint nor in the thing seen, but in the transversal, from one window to the other.

9. I, 644: "The specific pleasure of travel ... is to make the difference between departure and arrival not as imperceptible but as profound as possible, to experience it in its totality, intact...."

10. III, 545–46: "In physical suffering at least we do not have to choose our pain ourselves. Our disease determines it and imposes it upon us. But in jealousy, we must test in a sense every kind of suffering and every size before deciding on the one that seems likely to suit us."

11. Cf. the famous descriptions of sleep and waking, I, 3–9; II, 86–88.

12. III, 593. Here it is forgetting that has a power of fragmented interpolation, introducing distances between us and recent events, but in II, 757, it is memory that is interpolated and establishes the contiguity in distant things.

10. Levels of the Search

1. III, 615. And *Contre Sainte-Beuve*, chap. XIII.

2. III, 489: "In a crowd, these elements can ..."

3. Gide, militating for the rights of a homosexuality-as-logos, reproaches Proust for considering only cases of inversion and effeminacy. He thus remains on the second level and seems not to understand the Proustian theory at all. (The same is true of those who remain at the theme of guilt in Proust.)

4. This theme of profanation, so frequent in his work and his life, is generally expressed by Proust in terms of "belief": for example, I, 162–64. I believe it refers, rather, to an entire technique of contiguities, of partitionings and communications between sealed vessels.

5. To love without being loved: I, 927. To stop loving: I, 610–11; III, 173. To be harsh and to deceive the beloved: III, 111.

11. The Three Machines

1. III, 1033, 911: "But other features (such as inversion) may make it necessary for the reader to read in a certain way in order to read well; the author has no cause for offense here, but on the contrary, must grant the reader the greatest freedom, telling him: Look for yourself, see if you see better with this lens, or this one, or even this one."

2. *Selected Letters of Malcolm Lowry*, Lippincott, p. 66.

3. III, 900: "A man who is born sensitive and who has no imagination might all the same write admirable novels."

4. On the concept of production in its relations with literature, see Pierre Macherey, *Pour une théorie de la production littéraire*, Maspéro.

5. III, 879. Even memory, still too material, needs a *spiritual equivalent*: III, 374–75.

6. The organization of *Time Regained* from "the party at Mme de Guermantes's" is therefore as follows: (a) the order of reminiscences and singular essences as a first dimension of the work of art, III, 866–96; (b) transition to suffering and love by virtue of the requirements of the total work of art, III, 896–98; (c) the order of pleasures and sufferings, and their general laws, as the second dimension of the work of art, confirming the first, III, 899–917; (d) transition, return to the first dimension, III, 918–20; (e) the order of alteration and death, as third dimension of the work of art contradicting the first, but overcoming the contradiction, III, 921–1029; (f) the Book with its three dimensions, III, 1029–48.

7. On the ecstatic character of resonance, see II, 874–75.

8. See the splendid analysis by Michel Souriau, *La Matière, la lettre et le verbe, Recherches philosophiques*, III.

9. III, 889: "Had not nature herself, from this viewpoint, put me on the path of art, was not nature a beginning of art?"

10. See Joyce, *Stephen Hero*. We have seen that the same was true of Proust, and that, in art, essence itself determined the conditions of its incarnation, instead of depending on given natural conditions.

11. Umberto Eco, *L'Oeuvre ouverte* (Paris: Editions du Seuil), p. 231.

12. Style

1. III, 257. This is the very power of art: "By art alone, we can get outside ourselves, can know what others see in this universe that is not the same as ours and whose landscapes would have remained as unknown to us as those that may be on the Moon. Thanks to art, instead of seeing a single world, our own, we see it multiplied, and we have as many worlds at our disposal as there are original artists, worlds more different from each other than those that spin through infinity..." (III, 895–96).

2. Proust certainly read Leibniz, if only in school: Saint-Loup, in his theory of war and strategy, invokes a specific point of Leibnizian doctrine ("You remember that book of philosophy we were reading together at Balbec..."; II, 115–16). More generally, we have found that Proust's singular essences were closer to the Leibnizian monads than to Platonic essences.

3. *Contre Sainte-Beuve*, pp. 207–8 and 216: "unorganized style." The entire chapter insists on the *effects of literature*, analogous to veritable optical effects.

4. We should have to compare the Proustian conception of the image with other post-Symbolist conceptions: for example, Joyce's epiphany or Pound's imagism and vorticism. The following features seem to be shared: image as autonomous link between two concrete objects *insofar* as they are different (image, concrete equation); style, as multiplicity of viewpoints toward the same object and exchange of viewpoints toward several objects; language, as integrating and comprehending its own variations constitutive of a universal history and making each fragment speak according to its own voice; literature as production, as operation of effect-producing machines; explication, not as didactic intention but as technique of envelopment and development; writing as *ideogrammatic* method (with which Proust allies himself on several occasions).

5. In relation to psychoanalytic investigations, Félix Guattari has formed a very rich concept of "transversality" to account for communications and relations of the unconscious: see "La Transversalité," *Psychothérapie institutionelle*, no. 1.

6. See the great passages on art in the Search: communication of a work with a public (III, 895–96); communication between two works by one author, for example, the sonata and the septet (III, 249–57); communication between different artists (II, 327; III, 158–59).

Conclusion to Part II

1. Charlus's three speeches: I, 765–67; II, 285–96; II, 553–65.

Gilles Deleuze (1925–1995) was professor of philosophy at the University of Paris, Vincennes–St. Denis. With Félix Guattari, he coauthored *Anti-Oedipus, A Thousand Plateaus,* and *Kafka.* He was also the author of *The Fold, Cinema 1: The Movement-Image, Cinema 2: The Time-Image, Foucault, Kant's Critical Philosophy,* and *Essays: Critical and Clinical.* All of these books are published in English by the University of Minnesota Press.

Richard Howard has translated many books of French criticism, including works by Barthes, Foucault, and Todorov. His literary translations include, most recently, *Absinthe: A Novel* by Christophe Bataille and Stendhal's *The Charterhouse of Parma.* A poet and critic, he teaches in the School of the Arts at Columbia University.

PR 888 . S427 W45
→ Recovering your Story:
weinstein

PQ 2631. R63 A77387   / Z 789413
→ Prousts Deadline   The world of
cane   Proust

PQ 2631. R63 Z 545486 / A883
                              / Prousts way.

PQ 2631. R63 A 8624
→ The Proust Project

BL 42.5. US S25 REIJ
→ Prousts In Search of lost Time